ESSAYS ON
ABORIGINALISM

DR BRIAN ROBERTS

First published 2016 by Dr Brian Ross Roberts

Cairns, Australia

ISBN 978-0-9953824-0-4

eISBN 978-0-9953824-1-1

Copyright © Dr Brian Ross Roberts 2016

brianroberts.am@gmail.com

Edited by Erica Blythe

Cover and interior design by The Booktress

www.thebooktress.com

Front cover image sourced from NT Department of Education

Author Photograph

Frances Mocknick

"I read this book with great interest, finding it exceptionally clear-minded and full of suggestive ideas and parallels. I fear the times are not welcoming towards free thought, and many of the notions Dr Roberts has advanced that seem most worthwhile to me, are in the category of present day Australian heresy. I am struck by the way that modern experts tend not to recognise the ways in which they re-enact colonial patterns of engagement."

Nicolas Rothwell, award-winning author

"Brian has done us a great favour with his latest offering of essays on Aboriginal affairs. It is refreshing to read writing straight from the heart, without any axe to grind or agenda to push. He not only gets you thinking, but thinking in new ways. And new ways of thinking on Aboriginal affairs is precisely what we need."

Dr Anthony Dillon, Australian Catholic University

"Dr Roberts has an extraordinary capacity to grasp and hold onto the big picture while conducting a forensic examination of every facet of the Aboriginal debate. He writes with empathy to distinguish between the urban Aborigines and those who remain isolated and basically culturally unchanged, while highlighting the difficulties the Aboriginal cause has in speaking with one voice for constitutional change, recognition, equity and advancement."

Alec Lucke, Road to Exploitation: Political Capture by Mining in Queensland

"Dr Roberts' views are very broadly balanced because he cares both professionally and personally. His concern for the realism of management of culture in the future to continue to be authentic is genuine; for people of all cultures to manage their issues and cultural knowledge in the way their profound learnings have taught them. True culture brings balance in a way that our children of the future can feel free, affected by their cultural learning in a positive way, with great pride and dignity, that will always have a 'genuine fit within our changing world' because as Australians we are one and, we are many. Thank you always for your genuine caring through the important and clear messages within your big picture presentations. It would be sad if Indigenous students and staff did not study your positive, balanced Indigenous texts."

Jeannie Aileen Little, "Gaarkamunda" OAM

Other titles by Dr Brian Roberts

Professional Titles
Birth of Landcare
Call of the Country
Common Grasses of Orange Free State
Grasses of the Northern Cape, RSA
Ground Rules
Landcare Manual
Sustainable Agriculture and Land Use
Western Grasses, Queensland
Wildlife Management on Farms

Private Titles
Essays on Aboriginalism
Jean's Story
Lot 22: The Story of a Daintree Block
Overcoming Disadvantage
Son of the Veld
South Africa Revisited
Veld: Collected Papers 1956-1975
Where Angels Fear to Tread *(in press)*
Whitefella Dreaming

Dedicated to my wife, Margaret, whose resilience as home-maker, despite difficult health conditions, has grounded our family since 1956.

TABLE OF CONTENTS

PREFACE

The term Aboriginalism is used here in a similar way to Judaism, Socialism or Capitalism. It is in essence a system governed by principles grounded in First Peoples' values. Aboriginalism is a global phenomenon exhibited in many geographical regions, usually where climate and topography are not conducive to modern agriculture. In many cases, the societies displaying Aboriginalism have involuntarily contracted from more extensive original homelands, to their present locations. In other cases they involuntarily occupy locations reserved for Aboriginal people by the nationstate.

Aboriginality, i.e. being Aboriginal, cannot be studied or assessed in isolation, if it is to be properly understood as a subset of the Human Sciences. It is in the way that Aboriginality differs from other group identities, that its strengths and weaknesses are best evaluated and it is at the inter-cultural interface, that Aboriginality is best compared with other societal constructs.

The United Nations has produced a Declaration of Indigenous Rights, which acts as a touchstone for governments worldwide when they're confronted with Indigenous claims to land, human rights and autonomy. In the present compilation of essays, Aboriginalism in its Australian context, is analysed as a subset of a modern multicultural nation state. These essays were written over a period of two years and were constructed as stand-alone pieces for journal

1

publication. For this reason, the essays don't flow as a cohesive and sequential thought pattern but rather they attempt to unpack the societal impact of a range of Aboriginal-related topics.

Some Australian readers will wonder at the extent of South African material included in this essay collection. I believe that it is useful for Australian Aborigines to also view their situation through the African lens, if only to appreciate the comparative differences and similarities. This relativity also makes a change from the usual Australian comparison with the New Zealand and Canadian indigenes.

Some repetition of certain concepts is inevitable in a collection of stand-alone journal articles, so the author apologises up front if repetition irks some readers. However, it is hoped that these essays can be useful to secondary and tertiary teachers in their Humanities classes, since together they provide a nuanced range of liberal, conservative and Indigenous views on Australian race relations.

Since much of the original thinking on Australian Indigenous policy and principle stems from Noel Pearson, his writings are repeatedly referred to. Pearson however, is not judged as having all the answers, so he is challenged on a number of issues. As a knowledgeable ideas man, Pearson's well-articulated proposals carry more gravitas than those of any of his colleagues, with the possible exception of Marcia Langton.

The essays are grouped into six arbitrary subject areas, although logical sequencing within each part is problematic, it is hoped that this contribution will provide alternative views in the present debate on Indigenous Futures.

Brian Roberts
Cairns 2016

PART ONE
History and Origins

FIRST CONTACT:
A Historical Assessment

The Australian narrative of first contact between Indigenous people and exotic visitors has been described in many different ways: friendly, tentative, fierce and variations of these descriptions. Before revisiting the local contacts in Cape York, Western Australia, Tasmania and Botany Bay, it is instructive to compare these early encounters with those which predated the British by several centuries (Cummins, 2009). [see p.9]

The Phoenicians

A good starting point is the Phoenicians who are said to have circumnavigated Africa around 600 BC. They'd become a seafaring nation from about 1400 BC and can claim the title of the first maritime explorers the world had known. The earliest civilisations of Mesopotamia, then Egypt and Samaria, were followed by Assyria and Greece. If the Old Testament is correct, the Phoenicians may well have also reached the shores of India at a very early date. They were not primarily navigators, rather they were traders seeking to open up new markets along their new-found sea routes. Unlike later expeditionary forces, the Phoenicians were not empire-builders seeking to conquer new lands for their king, but came as commercial emissaries offering manufactured goods to more primitive peoples who lacked advanced technology. As a result, their first contacts were largely peaceful, which cannot be said for many successive seekers pursuing wealth and even human resources.

The Romans to Britannia

After several centuries of more localised maritime adventure, largely in the Mediterranean region, one of the next major contact zones was the Roman invasion of Britain in 55 BC. It must have been clear to the Celtic tribesmen that the vast fleet of ships was no ordinary trading mission. Julius Caesar had organised the loading of 10,000 legionnaires and 500 cavalry. He had conquered Gaul (France) and it was from there that his centurions had learned of the mystical Britannia, where semi-naked tribesmen rode horses and used small wickerwork chariots. This mystical island was said to be inhabited by primitive hairy people who fought among themselves as clans, each with their own king. As the Iron Age expanded to Britain, an increasing number of European clans of Celtic origin, migrated to Britain until fierce competition for arable land developed. So the Celts, Picts, Angels, Saxons and Gaelic clans, became warring factions. Some had become actively engaged in supporting the Gallic tribes against Caesar on the continent. (Well do I remember my 1948 Latin text book titled 'Caesar's Gallic Wars' – a chronicle of continuous strife.)

The Romans had heard of these bizarre blue-painted, wild-haired tribesmen with their javelins, daggers and long flat swords. Their feral reputation and untamable nature had gone before them, so when Caesar's men arrived for a second time in 54 BC they had 800 ships and 40,000 legionnaires whose linked armour could easily overcome the naked Celtic tribesmen. The legions soon overcame the palisaded hilltop forts of the Celts but Caesar left their king in charge provided they paid tribute to

Rome by way of annual taxes. This went on for nearly a hundred years until Emperor Claudius again invaded with a huge force, ruthlessly conquered the locals and took over their tin and iron mines together with their grain supplies. Over the next 400 years modern-day England was created.

In the process of Romanising the country, the mystical Druids were hunted down and eliminated, Queen Boudicca and her tribesmen were killed or enslaved, and the sacred groves of their religion were chopped down for timber. So began what the Romans saw as the civilisation of the British Isles, starting with roads, cities, ship-yards and a vast trading network with Europe and the Mediterranean. Over time, the local tribes became more educated, more technologically advanced and more productive in their agriculture and mining. At the same time their animistic religion, centred on sites such as Stonehenge, were replaced by the coming of Christianity via Ireland and the new monasteries. It is often asked how long it might have taken the tribesmen of Britannia to become a truly civilised nation if the Romans had not contributed their significant leap forward.

The Norsemen, Vikings, Columbus and Cortez

After the Roman excursions to Britain, the next major explorations were those of the Norsemen and Vikings from about 860AD. Rather than militant raiders, these Scandinavians were usually farmers seeking new land in Greenland, Scotland and Vinland (North-Eastern North America). Then in 1492 Columbus arrived in the Caribbean, followed by Cortez in 1519 who came up against Montezuma's Incas.

The first circumnavigation of the globe, completed in 1521, was the Magellan/Elcano three-year voyage. From 1539 De Soto travelled up the Mississippi and De Orellano explored the Amazon and by 1606 the English had entered Virginia.

The Dutch in the East Indies

Australia becomes known to the world when it is 'discovered' by the Dutch in 1623, unaware that the Aborigines had been here for at least 50,000 years. This discovery is actually predated by the Spaniard De Torres who sailed further South than his predecessors in search of the Unknown Southland. De Torres was the first European to enter the strait which now bears his name, between New Guinea and Australia. The Spanish would keep this shortcut to the Philippines secret for the next 150 years. It was the Dutch, under Willelm Janszoon in his Dutch East India Company (VOC) ship the 'Duyfken' in 1605 who first made contact with the natives of Australia at Cape Keerweer (Turn again) on the West coast of Cape York, North of present-day Weipa. This first encounter was hostile, with Aborigines preventing the Dutch from landing to take on water and fresh food. Janszoon returned to Holland unimpressed by this featureless hostile place.

Then in 1623, the Dutch Jan Carstensz re-traced much of Janszoon's route and made landfall on the same coast as his predecessor. He left us the very first recorded description of the local inhabitants of Western Cape York. It is important to note that Carstensz' instructions from the VOC were to bring back [preferably] young boys or girls who could be 'broken in', possibly for use as interpreters. But Carstensz was a slave hunter, not an explorer in the normal sense. At first he tried to entice the Aborigines out of the coastal forest by leaving pieces of iron and strings of beads on a stick, but the Aborigines didn't respond. A few days later two parties of men went ashore in the ship's boats. This time the armed blacks showed no fear and touched the muskets of the Dutch, trying to remove them from the men's shoulders. The English translation of Carstensz's report reads: 'Our men accordingly diverted their attention by showing them the iron and beads, and espying vantage, seized one of the blacks by a string which he wore around his neck and carried him off to the pinnace (long boat). The blacks who remained on the beach, set up dreadful howls. These natives are coal-black with lean bodies and [are] stark-naked, having twisted baskets or nets around their heads. In hair and figure, they are like the blacks of the Coromandel (Indian) coast, but they seem to be less cunning, bold and evil-natured than the blacks of the Western extremity of Nova Guinea (today's Irian Jaya).'

Joseph Cummins in his book *First Encounters* (2009) adds a note of caution to readers' assessment of Carstensz as a mariner of his day (1620's): 'He comes across in his journals as an ugly figure, with far more than his share of the racism of his age.' Marching inland he and his men 'found great quantities of diverse human bones from which it may be concluded that the blacks [of the area] are man-eaters who do not spare each other when driven by hunger.' (Cummins maintains that Carstensz thought he was in New Guinea and that the Aborigines were head-hunters.) Two hundred Aborigines gathered and attacked the Dutchmen, who shot one of the attackers. The Aborigines fled and Carstensz was able to inspect one of their deserted huts and to report that: 'The natives are utter barbarians...It may safely be concluded that they are poor and abject wretches.' He then adds for the record: 'In all the places we have landed we have treated the blacks or savages with especial kindness, offering them [trinkets], hoping that by so doing, to get their friendship. But in spite of all our kindness and semblance, the blacks received us as enemies everywhere, so that in most places our landings were attended with great peril.'

Next on the Australian contact scene was Dirk Hartog, also of the VOC, but this time coming ashore at the other side of the Unknown Southland, at Shark bay on the coast of Western Australia. Hartog and his successor Francois Pelsaert (1629) liked to refer to this continent as New Holland for it was the last landfall before reaching their East Indies capital Batavia (today's Jakarta). After a series of murders among the shipwrecked Dutch on the Abrolhos Islands, fifty miles off the mainland, Pelsaert rowed forty-eight survivors to the WA coast in search of water and food. They spied eight black men who fled as soon as the Dutchmen with muskets came near them. Eventually the Dutchmen found water and crayfish, then rowed all the way to their kinsmen in Batavia. (While working in Indonesia in the 1980's, I was fascinated to find a Dutch castle on the island of Sulawesi which so closely resembled the Cape Town castle built by Jan Van Riebeeck in 1653, that it seemed probable that both were designed by the same Dutch architect.)

Next came Abel Tasman, also of the VOC, who made the first serious attempt to map New Holland, leaving Batavia in early 1642 and sailing West to Mauritius, Tasman then veered so far South that icebergs became a major threat to his small ships. Turning North, he eventually came in sight of what he named Van Diemen's Land after the head of the VOC. Later he was honoured by it being re-named Tasmania. While Tasman was the first European to set eyes on Tasmania, he didn't come across any Aborigines, who'd been there for 10,000 years. He'd heard what seemed to be human sounds, but no contact was made with the Tasmanians until the French arrived and skirmished with the locals in 1772. What impressed Tasman most was the enormous size of the local trees, but having noted the rugged nature of Van Diemen's Land, he sailed East for two weeks before becoming the first European to set eyes on New Zealand. Travelling up the West coast of South Island he came to the gap between the South and North Islands. He anchored at a beach in the gap and was met by thirteen Maori warriors in a giant canoe. 'These people apparently sought our friendship,' recorded Tasman, unaware that he was the first White to contact Polynesian seafarers who'd been in Maoriland for over 400 years. Before long, the Dutch invitation to come aboard their ship was declined. Instead, the Maori, in a double-prowed outrigger, rammed the Dutch ship's longboat and killed three of the newcomers, leading Tasman to name the place Murderer's Bay, known later as Cook Strait.

In assessing Tasman's encounter, Cummins describes this as 'a classic first contact clash between two cultures. The Maori recognised the large ship with armed men as an obvious invading force and saw fit to attack without warning'. The Dutch, although they did intend to take over the islands and named them New Zealand (or Nieu Zeeland), were not planning an early attack, only an assessment of the land's potential for trade. Tasman returned to Holland, reporting that there was not much to be found in Tasmania and that the New Zealand natives were unusually fierce. He made no report on the Unknown Southland as such.

The French in Asia

Although Louis-Antoine de Bougainville, was not involved in the discovery of Australia, his arrival from France in 1768 on the shores of Tahiti is recorded as one of the more important contacts between Pacific Islanders and Europeans. These islands had been settled by the Polynesian voyagers sometime between 300 and 800 AD. The land, vegetation, mountains, streams and particularly the people, were the most beautiful Bougainville's 400 sailors had seen in all their travels. As soon as the French had anchored, their ships were surrounded by a fleet of naked young women in canoes. These Pacific Venuses boarded the ships and nimbly climbed the rigging, leaving Bougainville wondering however he would be able to keep his men at work. He noted the lighter skin colour of these people and how different they were from the darker and larger 'savages' he'd met elsewhere. He was so besotted with these beautiful peaceful people that he never got to know many other home truths about Tahitian society – incest, infanticide, a strict caste system and enslavement of their neighbours. Perhaps unsurprisingly, it wasn't long before pick-pocketing, petty theft and demand for food, iron, glass and fabric, led to a souring of relations. Bougainville was not to know that the Tahitian population of 50,000 was to drop to 16,000 in the next 30 years as a result of venereal disease, smallpox, typhus and influenza, aggravated by alcohol-fuelled violence. His Garden of Eden was no more.

It is worth noting that this Tahitian experience seemed like living proof of the 'Noble Savage' concept, first put forward by the French philosopher Jean-Jacques Rousseau in 1750. In essence, this theory postulates that: 'men and women living in utopian primitive societies [are] protected by their innocence' (Cummins). Rousseau believed that man in his natural Edenic state was good, but that he had been corrupted by civilisation through its religion, money, property and materialism generally. In the end, it was European diseases rather than the trappings of modernity, which ended the noble innocence.

Cook's British Endeavour

Finally we come to the contact of James Cook with the Aborigines, leaving aside the great incursions into South America by the Spaniards and Portuguese. While Australians are all aware of Cook's journey up the East coast of their continent, his meetings with the Maori are less well known here. In mid 1769 Cook's 'Endeavour' anchored in Mercury Bay on New Zealand's North Island. He had brought scientists from London's Royal Society to record the passage of the planet Venus as it passed before the sun. The sightings would be from the nearby island of Tahiti where Cook had set up the scientists' camp.

The Maori of the North Island had originally paddled from the Polynesian Islands several centuries before, but had never seen ships as large as the Endeavour. A young Maori boy named Te Horeta lived long enough to tell the story of first contact with Whites in the next century. The ship, he said, was taken for a massive bird or even a floating island. The Maori elders decided that it had come from the Spirit World, an impression which seemed to be confirmed by the whiteness of the people who came ashore. The warriors watched the landing party warily, while the children fled into the forest. The white skin, fair hair and blue eyes of the newcomers fascinated the Maori, who offered Cook's men fish and roots which were ravenously eaten by the sailors. Cook offered them salt meat in return, but the Maori spat it out. Te Horeta recalled: 'the meat's saltiness ripped our throats.' (Which is also probably why many sailors preferred to catch bilge rats!)

When a sailor brought down a flying bird with his gun, the Maori were astounded, but when one of them 'stole' a seaman's coat without giving anything in return, he was shot dead. The Maori then understood the power of firearms but didn't blame the sailor, because the warrior had stolen the coat and offered nothing in return. The Maori left, but Te Horeta was invited to stay on board and be examined very closely before being given an iron nail as his special gift from the Whites. He was to treasure it for the rest of his long life.

After recording the passage of Venus, Cook set sail for what he was really interested in, searching for the Southern continent. He followed Admiralty orders and sailed toward 40 degrees South until he hit the cold and stormy Roaring Forties. The mountainous seas caused one of the scientists to record: 'We could get no rest or scarcely lie in bed.' Cook wrote: 'We had no prospect of meeting land', so he followed his next order which was to sail West until he sighted Van Dieman's Land, found by Tasman a century earlier, then to ascertain whether that land was in fact part of *Terra Australis*. After about a month, Cook seemed to have given up hope, writing: 'As to a Southern Continent, I do not believe such a thing exists, unless at a high latitude.'

He dreaded having to return home via the Cape of Good Hope (Cape Town). After nineteen days of sailing North-West he sighted land which he thought was Tasmania but was in fact the coast of present-day Victoria. Cook sailed North, surveying the coast, landing first at Botany Bay (present-day Sydney) and claimed the land for the British Crown.

Cook found that his Tahitian interpreter was of no help at all in understanding the Aborigines. He approached the Aborigines with gifts of nails which were thrown to them, but the locals saw this as a threat and threw a spear at the shore party. Cook ordered a shot to be fired in the air, upon which the Aborigines shouted '*Warra Warra Wai*' which Cook later found to mean 'go away'. Somewhat puzzled, Cook recorded: 'All they seemed to want was for us to be gone.' He sailed North, mapping the coast and naming prominent features until he reached Cape Tribulation North of present-day Cairns.

At 10pm on 11ᵗʰ June 1770, the Endeavour ran aground on the inner Barrier Reef. After jettisoning 20 tons of canon, stone ballast and iron, she rode out on the high tide. Cook temporarily stopped the leaks with sailcloth under the hull and drew his ship up on the beach of what he named the Endeavour River at present-day Cooktown. Cook goes down in history as the first European to sight what the locals called a 'kanguru'. The Aborigines however, were very disturbed by the large number of their turtles which the crew were capturing, so they set fire to the grass to scare the crew off. Cook responded with musket-fire, but soon after, having completed his ship's repairs, he sailed among the coral reefs to the tip of Cape York where he landed, raised the Union Jack and recorded: 'I now once more hoisted the British Colours in the name of King George III.' He took possession of the whole Eastern Coast and named it New South Wales.

He returned on a second voyage after eighteen months, to navigate the waters near Antarctica, then undertook his final voyage of discovery in search of the North-West Passage, sailing through the icy Bering Strait. In 1779 he was returning home via Hawaii when he was killed by the natives at Kealakekua Bay, while trying to recover one of the ship's boats stolen by the natives.

First Contact in Retrospect

In view of the persistent and evidence-based claim by today's Aboriginal peoples that they have been dispossessed and deserve recompense or compensation, it is useful to compare the position of Australian Aborigines with other global indigenous peoples and their claims to self-government and sovereignty. In no case have the colonisers admitted their illegal occupation and withdrawn soon after invasion, leaving the original occupants to re-group and rebuild their First Nation untrammelled by intruders. However, in the 1800's and 1900's, several colonising powers withdrew and today 'de-colonisation' has become the buzzword of choice when referring to reclamation of previous status. While this concept implies reverse colonisation, all parties appear to agree that getting back to the pre-colonial situation is neither possible nor desirable. So the first question is: 'How different would the Aborigines' position be today, had the colonial powers entered into an early Treaty, or proclaimed an Annexation or Ceding of this new colony? Many of today's Aboriginal leaders insist that their people never gave up their sovereignty, never ceded their land to the invaders and never signed up for any agreement by which their level of land ownership was diminished. They are correct. The inference from all this, is that the First People remain a sovereign nation with full independent rights.

It is good to remind ourselves of the Colonial Office's orders to governors in Britain's overseas territories in the early 1800's: Native peoples were to be given full rights to hunt and live in their accustomed manner, and the rights of pastoral lessees of Crown land were limited to the grazing of domestic stock. At stake was the limited right to act as sole occupier of rural land where Aborigines retained the full 'usufruct' of their tribal land.

The important point here is that this Aboriginal right was never rescinded, but somehow when the Australian Federation created Aboriginal Reserves, the States took it upon themselves to cancel all Aboriginal land rights outside these Reserves. The invaders had conveniently forgotten or ignored Captain Cook's first report stating: 'All they seemed to want was for us to be gone.' Empire-builders were never put off by the locals' displeasure or minor resistance and they only sought treaties when their take-over met with serious opposing might.

A fitting way to end this essay is to leave ourselves with a few imponderables; the 'What If?' questions of alternative histories of the 'Unknown South Land':

- What if no Europeans ever found this country? Where would the Aborigines be today?
- What if Portugal or Spain had settled this continent?
- What if the Chinese mariners of the 1400's had established their New China here? How would they have protected Aboriginal Rights?
- What if the British had signed a Waitangi (NZ)-type Treaty? Would the Aborigines have the political power of the Maori today?

And for the future:

- What if Australia approves Aboriginal Sovereignty?
- What if Aborigines can be convinced that modern urbanisation is the only moral prime objective for future generations?
- What if future mainstream Australians enculturate Aboriginal natural spirituality as a means of achieving mental stability and meaning?

Worth thinking about.

THE KHOI SAN BUSHMEN:
Oldest and Most Oppressed

Background

We live in an era when the rights and values of minorities are constantly on the political agenda but not high on the agenda. Presently there is a conflation of Australian and South African racial and political situations concerning the position of indigenous minorities; in Australia, the Aborigines make up 3% of the nation's population. They repeatedly claim significance because they believe that they're the world's oldest continuing culture and have illegally been dispossessed. In South Africa and neighbouring Namibia, the actual oldest people, the Khoi San Bushmen, have at last been scientifically recognised as carriers of probably[1] the most ancient human genome. Currently the basis of racist policies which discriminate against indigenous minorities are having their historic credentials re-examined and evaluated.

The Bushmen

When I was a boy in 1930's South Africa we would marvel at the Bushmen's cave paintings under the cliffs of the Kei River in the Eastern Cape Province. Later I studied books on such paintings found all over the mighty Drakensburg range. These were largely depictions of 'stick people' often with oversized buttocks, and of a range of animals identifiable by their horns. These people had been

[1] The other contender is the Hadza tribe of Tanzania.

in Southern Africa thousands of years before the southern migration of the larger more warlike Bantu who later formed the Zulu and Xhosa nations. (Interestingly these are the tribes of President Zuma and Mandela respectively).

Black-on-black dispossession has never been given much air-time in modern politics, so it is unsurprising that President Zuma has never admitted to the way his Zulus hunted and killed the Bushmen, taking the women and children as slaves to the Zulus. Nor was anyone surprised when in the New South Africa, the Bushmen were kept in their desert 'homeland' of the Kalahari Desert as if that was their preferred cultural environment. Nobody in the governing African National Congress (ANC) acted to bring equality to this small minority of hunter-gatherers (and later hunter-herders). The evidence from a thousand delicate cave paintings throughout Zululand never came before the courts to prove the claims of the real First People in Southern Africa. Is it not clear that hunter-gatherers migrate to, and settle, where the game is most abundant and most hunted? The game in turn migrate, to where fodder is most prevalent, and fodder in turn, is most productive where rainfall is conducive to herbage production. This is why desert was the least optimal for early humans and why, as tribes competed for resources, the weakest ended up with the driest country.

The most recent findings of Professor Vanessa Hayes, a South African paleo-geneticist now at the Garvan Institute in Australia, have at least settled the claims of 'oldest living culture', at least for now. What Hayes did was to extend her earlier genetic work to three tribes or groups of Khoi San people, to be able to compare the DNA of Bushmen living three different lifestyles. These studies allowed the identification of genes which may hold promise for contemporary medical science.

Hayes's extensive fieldwork brought strong evidence on two criteria which had long been contested by anthropologists and geneticists:

i.   The Khoi San people exhibited genomes (DNA patterns) which were at least 170,000 years old.

ii. The diversity of DNA in their blood was probably the world's most diverse because it was so ancient.

This combination of genomic traits arguably held greater potential for curing modern ailments than any other blood. Hayes claims that the Khoi San genome can now be regarded as the 'Genetic Baseline' of all humans, based on the 'Out of Africa' theory of origin and migration. Her contention is that we now have a scientific picture of the genetic make-up of what she terms 'Mitochondrial Eve', i.e. the original female DNA of *Homo sapiens* and *H. erectus* before her.

The fact that present-day Bushmen can go seven days without water but have no immunity to European diseases, points to significant differences in survival capacity of old and new humans. It has long been known that the Bushmen have the unique capacity to store fat and fluid in their pronounced buttocks and that their shaded eyelids and vaginal cover, give them added protection against harsh climates. It appears that European DNA contains only about 20% of the diversity of these ancient hunters and as a result, the European reference genome can't be used as a standard for earlier peoples due to the mismatch of gene-sequencing and the presence of ancient genes.

The Aboriginal Situation

Anthropologists have increasingly pushed back the age of Australia's First People. Mungo Man (actually a woman) was discovered after wind erosion exposed a fine-boned human skeleton in Western NSW in 1969. Before that discovery by Tim Bolger, estimates approximating 10,000 years were generally agreed as the earliest migrations of Aboriginal ancestors, possibly from Southern India, as an offshoot of the Dravidian[2] tribes. Estimates of the rate of human migrations, which suggest several kilometres per year, are not very useful when the effect of the most recent Ice Age in halting the largest migrations is taken into account. Many anthropologists hold that former migrations may only have re-commenced 20,000 years ago. Certainly the evidence of a series of different migratory peoples reaching this continent predates Post-Ice Age sea level rises. Equally telling is Birdsell's evidence of at least three distinct human types entering the Great Southland before and after landbridges to the north were available.

While the science behind migration theory is probably of minimal interest to present-day mainstream Australians, the political gravitas of 'world's oldest' claims is largely dependent on the comparable facts between continents. Obviously the Aboriginal claim that their ancestors outdate the European cultures by many millennia is well established. However, when political opportunism pushes factual claims beyond scientific credibility on a global scale, it is time for a re-assessment of claims based on sloppy mythology.

Why honesty in the dating of ancestry is important in contemporary Australia, is that outlandish claims to antiquity are being used as a political weapon to value-add to land claims and other real and fabricated narratives in the equity debate.

The time for separation of myth from fact is now, so that contemporary Australians have an accurate basis for their Referendum vote on Constitutional change.

---

[2] Munda and Dasa

SECRET RIVER
SECRETS

The TV documentary, 'Secret River' based on Kate Grenville's book of the same title, is worthy of serious consideration by our policy makers. Part 1, screened on ABC on 14/06/2015, started with the unjust and inhumane treatment of British convicts. The depravity of early Sydney under the control of the Rum Corp reflects the deficiencies of the first Whites to contact the Blacks.

When William Thornhill, representing Kate Grenville's ancestor, manages to acquire a small block of bush on the banks of the Hawkesbury, near present-day Wisemans Ferry, his young family is faced with impossible odds, as the complex white/black relations became the central theme. Thornhill was a Thames waterman, he knew all about boats, nothing about 'savages', but he was determined to carve a permanent niche out of the Australian bush for his growing family.

Predictably, Kate Grenville's narrative of her family research, was going to concentrate on the fate of the Thornhills, rather than on the position of the Aborigines. This didn't stop critics like Inga Clendinnen from deriding Kate's narrative as insensitive to the Black situation and the values which went with it. Grenville quite rightly steered clear of native viewpoints which she had no background to, but the film makes it clear that her ancestor recognised that his block wasn't *terra nullius* when he came upon the outline of a fish etched into a flat rock near his newly-completed cabin.

The film depicts an obvious clash of land ownership; one a colonial freehold title, the other an ancient hunter-gatherer claim. Despite the conflict between the males in the story, when Thornhill's wife Sal becomes seriously ill, an Aboriginal woman brings an eel as antidote to her affliction. When she recovers and Thornhill has to leave to continue working as a waterman at Sydney docks, she is again befriended by an Aboriginal woman who instructs her in bush tucker and other survival skills.

No doubt the local Darug people, the original inhabitants of the Hawkesbury, will have their own views on whether their mob has been fairly portrayed. The director of the two-part mini-series, Stephen Luby, apparently wanted others 'to experience the insight and empathy' which Kate's narrative had evoked in him.

A poignant moment, reflecting great political significance, is when Thornhill first surveys his new Utopia and frantically stabs four sticks into the grass, decisively proclaiming his newfound boundaries. Perhaps this message is largely lost on most viewers, but the racial conflict in this case is not caused by settlers fouling waterholes or dispersing food-source game or usurping women, as is repeatedly referred to in history books. Nor did the Aborigines spear the settlers' sheep, threaten women and children or burn down homesteads. Here we have a simple land ownership conflict, with both parties convinced that they have a clear legal and moral case.

As a narrative, Secret River portrays many historical and racial aspects of the contemporary over-sensitive and politically-correct framing of our history. The director captures the warts-and-all rawness of convict and Aboriginal life. The era within which the story is set is pre-missionaries, pre-schools, pre-reserves and pre-land rights. As such, it avoids the current all-pervasive arguments about lack of respect and fairness from invaders. To that extent, Secret River tells it as it was in the first decade at Botany Bay – no stolen generation, no protectors, no native police, no anthropologists, no Perkins, Pearson, Dodson or Langton. No, this is the unadulterated first contact, the unrehearsed clash of the world's most and least advanced peoples. The native spirituality shines through, as does the natural fit of the natives into the landscape and their incredulity that anyone else could claim to own their ancestors' land.

In this historic 'square-one' point in time, it is informative to debate how things may have turned out differently 'if only'. If only the natives had made themselves useful as co-operative co-workers in progressing the new enlightenment. If only the settlers had respected native customs, antiquity and spirituality. If only the NSW Government had respected London's insistence that the natives retain their right to use land and waters as they always had done. If only the whites had valued the blacks' evolutionary situation. If only land administrators had been guided by a Treaty. If only the natives had developed powerful bows and poison arrows as the Khoi San Bushman of Africa had. If only the first settlers were as educated and understanding as some of the later pastoralists on Queensland's Cooper Creek whose appreciation of natives' knowledge and culture led to peaceful co-habitation.

Part 2 of Secret River starts by showing the friendly side of early race relations; Sal being taught all about bush tucker and the kids learning to play spear throwing with the young Aborigines. The little Londoners in turn, demonstrate their kite-flying skills. Both sets of skills expose the 'otherness' of the contact groups. Viewers are left in no doubt that there exists a basic sociability and mutual helpfulness on both sides, at least among women and children.

Unfortunately the men are very different. Wil is convinced that he has legal title to his land. He'd be glad if the natives would just get off his place, but unsurprisingly the local leader stands firm: 'This has always been our land.' Wil sails to Sydney, is offered two convict labourers and buys himself a big new gun – for shooting kangaroos, he says.

The film makes a point of demonstrating how well the natives fit into the landscape, how they live off kangaroos, goannas and fish, and how they make friction fire – an art which Wil's son learns and shows to his dad. Then the Thornhills host a gathering of their few neighbours. They talk of the local savages, and one suggests that they're like children and should be treated as such. Slasher Sullivan, the wild Irishman from down river, who shoots at every savage he sees, regales the group with tales of cannibalism, cutting a pregnant white woman open and devouring her foetus. Slasher says there's money on blacks' skulls, which are sought after by scientists. Slasher then rips off his shirt to reveal the horrendous raised flail-scars on his back, making the point that his hatred of the Rum Corp is deep-seated and vengeful. Blackwater, the settlement official, reminds the group that the natives were friendly at first, but they don't trust the whites after many betrayals and land-grabs. He advises Wil to leave the locals alone and they will reciprocate – but that's not Wil's experience, although he seems to accept Blackwater's advice of 'take a little, give a little' as the basis for peace.

Out of the blue we see a whole squadron of longboats, packed with Redcoats and flying Union Jacks, rowing up the Hawkesbury toward Wil's place. A fire starts near his house, then a confusion of shots, shouts and curses leaves the whole Aboriginal mob in tatters. One convict is speared, an Aboriginal family is found poisoned with arsenic-laced flour and a new uneasy calm descends on the valley.

The film ends with close-up shots of Wil, in a smart buttoned smock-coat plus high white collar and high boots, having his portrait painted as the Lord of Cobham Hall, a huge grandly laid-out manor house plus estate garden. Sal, now lady of the house, is fussed-about by uniformed maids at her service. The final scene shows them on their verandah, both dressed to the nines, surveying their grand estate. Sal appears to have lost her insistence on returning to the sound of Bow Bells, and Wil looks more than a little smug with his accomplishments, even if they were at a huge human cost to the Aborigines who stole the corncobs from his first crop.

Viewers are left with images of an uncomfortable and superficial white population with a tenuous grip on newly-grabbed land which continues to threaten them and which gives contemporary Australians a renewed challenge to their identity. So the 'Who are we?' question remains only superficially answered.

AUSTRALIA'S
BRAVE WARRIORS

For a couple of decades now, the Australian mainstream and the Aboriginal minority have increasingly been at odds on just who our war memorials should honour. As a fair-minded nation who are willing to give credit where credit is due, there has been a reluctance to include Aborigines in both the mateship of comrades sharing full rights including soldier-settler blocks, and the sacred remembrance of memorials.

After the 'Empire' historians had dominated Australian history for decades, Henry Reynolds whose grandmother is Aboriginal, was the first to put the colonial record straight. His several books on Rights, Sovereignty, and Colonial Trauma were overshadowed by his 'The Other Side of the Frontier' (1981), which was published over three decades ago. Equally telling, is Reynolds' 'Why Didn't They Tell Us', which is a serious indictment to the Australian education system and its one-eyed historians. Geoffrey Blainey's 'Triumph of the Nomads' went some way toward encouraging a bifocal view, but it was the comparison of the 'Three Cheers' view of our history, with the 'Black Armband' view, which eventually gained some traction, at least in the press.

The bold attempt by Keating to wake up the nation to the reality of dispossession, in his seminal Redfern speech in December 1992, was followed by a push in the opposite direction by Howard's resurrection of Menzies-era historical priorities. In recent years we have had several worthy attempts to re-position Aboriginal history, culture and tradition in the Australian psyche. Two examples of this are Bill Gammage's 'The World's Greatest Estate', and Bruce Pascoe's 'Dark Emu', both of which bring evidence to support an increasing awareness of early Aboriginal sophistication, so misunderstood by the 'oppressive invaders'. The archaeologist Josephine Flood quotes Claude Levi Strauss as concluding that 'Australian Aborigines were the intellectual aristocrats among [the world's] early peoples'. Flood's studies demonstrate that their outstanding features included 'a sophisticated religion, art and social organisation, an egalitarian system of both justice and decision-making, a complex far-flung trading network and an ability to adapt and survive in some of the world's harshest environments.'

In mid 2015 Libby Connors of USQ in Toowoomba, produced her remarkable tribal history of southern coastal Queensland, titled 'Warrior'. This is a well-researched account of a young Aboriginal leader, lawman and warrior named Dundalli of the Dalla people whose country was north of, and inland from Moreton Bay. Of special interest in Connors' approach, is the way she explains the conflicting interactions between government and squatters, Aborigines and missionaries and between competing tribes vying for support from the three centres of White power. Rather than the good guy/bad guy dichotomy which is so commonly used by our history writers, Connors does a fair job at encouraging the reader to put themselves in the shoes of each of the conflicted groups, though she seldom fails to empathise with the dispossessed tribes. Her archival detective work is minutely referenced, as she also draws heavily on a few previous recorders of Brisbane history. Perhaps the most striking feature of Connors' research is the insightful way in which she explains the internal processes by which the tribal people took decisions on how to respond to White interference in its many forms.

It could have been predicted that the literary critics would have tackled the author on the way she presumes much, but often on little evidence. So when one critic says it is 'clearly just informed fiction – there are no records to attest to any of it', the reader needs to get the historical record into perspective. This is why the same critic (Weekend Australian 23/05/2015) admits that well-informed speculation 'is the only tool available to the historian'. In the absence of records of Aboriginal values, priorities, responses, considerations and both group and individual motivations, no author has done better than Connors at explaining, on the basis of probability, how Aboriginal reaction to White aggression was considered, discussed, decided upon and enacted. The way in which tribal councils nominated chosen individuals to implement their decisions, will be an eye-opener to many mainstreamers, whose school history depicts a disorganised rabble of treacherous cannibalistic savages as a barrier to the enlightenment of the Australian continent by brave educated Christians.

Connors does a remarkably rational job of convincing the reader, that when the local tribes initially allowed the settlers onto their land, it was on the clear understanding that all would share in the new arrangement. Their reasoning was: we give you grazing and water and a place for your homestead, you give us a share of the animals and crops produced on our land. You have your women and children and we have ours. Together we will defend our partnership's resources against intruders, Black and White. Connors apparently was unable to find any record of acceptance of this sharing concept by the Whites, so when the Blacks helped themselves to the odd sheep or cow or row of corn, the punishable act of theft was seen for what the British regarded it as.

From there on, the game of payback was on for young and old and the schoolyard claim of 'he started it', became the crux of never-ending court cases. The fact that the Aboriginal peoples were sovereign, didn't occur to the newcomers or, if it did, was judiciously ignored as what today is called an 'inconvenient truth'. Neither did it occur to the government, judiciary, squatters or police, that the well-considered decisions on reprisals were made on the basis of tribal law. Respondents were in fact duty-bound by their law to respond in the same measure as they would to misdemeanors by neighbouring tribes who took their women, their waterholes or their kangaroos. Whoever disrespected their legal code must suffer the well-respected consequences.

The fundamental problem lay in the government's failure to negotiate, failure to contemplate that a Treaty would offer a clear and fair agreement on land and rights generally. Connors doesn't say this, but all her detailed records of court cases and sentences, indicate that the British, as they had on other continents, played the 'Might is Right' game. This is why when they came up against large well-organised militaries in Africa and New Zealand, Treaties and Conventions replaced Annexations and Royal Claims.

Connors is perhaps the first historian to point out to the great-unwashed descendants of the imperial colonist that Aboriginal law ensured that both contesting parties were satisfied. How this compares with *Magna Carta* and Westminster, is for others to judge, but in practice, the ignoring of Aboriginal rights formed the basis of British 'progressive justice'. She describes how early contact led to the Dalla people bringing generous supplies of bark for roofing settlers' cottages, in return for iron, glass, flour and beef. However, when ex-convict shepherds interfered with the Dalla women, reprisal was swift and spearing of shepherds led in turn, to poisoning of the attackers with arsenic-laced flour or meat. The starting point of this repeated vicious cycle seems to almost always have been the Whiteman's unwillingness to share.

The Dalla regarded the stock which had appeared on their age-old cultural domain, as a new resource. When an Aboriginal stockman pointed out a beast to a station manager, saying: 'That fellow belonging to me and you', it was clear what he meant. In welcoming the first settlers onto their land, the Dalla had never considered a change of land ownership to their ancestral country. They had nurtured escaped convicts and surviving castaways, they had even taken them into the tribe as 'brothers.' In time, these White fringe-dwellers were perhaps the first to appreciate the inherent 'mateship' of the locals and in several instances these untutored Whites played a vital role in getting the White legal system to consider the indigenous law and the obligation it placed on individuals. The courts never did understand honourable payback by the tribesmen fighting to retain their land. Nor did the courts ever accept sovereign land ownership by the original peoples.

It is this 'Rule Britannia' view of lesser mortals, which is at the heart of Connors' thesis. While her Morton Bay microcosm is her focus, Connors is well aware of the way this assumed English superiority had at least temporarily subdued the tribes of Africa, India and the New World. She sees the tribal councils' eventual plan for all-out war against the intruders, as a predictable consequence of widespread and intensifying injustice toward the First Peoples. So when the tribes between the sea and mountains planned to block the inland roads, spear the White bosses and starve out the squatters on the Darling Downs, this is regarded by Connors as a natural and justified last-ditch stand by the dispossessed tribesmen.

As a historian, Connors is at a loss to understand why there is still no official lasting recognition of the Brisbane frontier conflict. Lasting from 1824 to 1865, this was Australia's longest frontier 'war'. At the centre of the conflict was one warrior, Dundalli, whose bravery, integrity, and negotiating ability, drew thousands of his countrymen into untold skirmishes on the basis of their law, when all else failed. Surely, asks Connors, the Australian legend should have a place of honour for such patriots. By such omissions, the ANZAC tradition is tarnished and becomes but a poor substitute for what the truly inclusive Australian narrative should be.

A final comment on Connors' unique attempt to weigh the colonial scales of justice, should include her introductory statement that biased sources make telling of Dundalli's story difficult but not impossible. Who, one might ask, could have recorded an unbiased assessment of this warrior's merits or otherwise? Herein lies the challenge for would-be authors, to do what Connors has done, for their people in the Kimberley, in Arnhemland, in the Gulf, in Cape York and even in the now urbanised areas of Victoria and New South Wales. Australia needs to hear the real histories of Jandamara and other warriors who fought the good fight for the most justifiable of all causes – our people's country. As the old poem 'The Man Who Counts' ends:

And if he should lose
His place will never be
Amongst those timid souls
Who knew neither victory nor defeat.

WHERE YOU FROM BROTHER?

The usual answer to this question from one Aborigine to another, would be Kuku Yalangi country or Yolngu country or some other clan country. However, few individuals seem to be aware that they too are migrants, albeit ancient migrants. To dispel the vague idea that they arose from Lake Mungo or from Kow Swamp, it is useful to re-examine the best evidence of the origins of Australia's first humans, who all appear to have been *Homo sapiens* rather than the 'sub-human' *Homo erectus* as some early anthropologists suggested.

In a masterful overview entitled 'The Original Australians' (2006) Josephine Flood has summarised the evidence to date, on where present-day Aborigines actually began their journey to what the mariners of the 1600's referred to as The Great Southland. The long-accepted 'Out of Africa' theory holds that about 150,000 years ago (k y a) humans spread from North Africa across the globe and in the process, *H. erectus* replaced earlier sub-types with a minimum of genetic mixing. Since the 1980's, DNA studies have shed new light on human migrations, in this case indicating a common origin of New Guineans and Australians. The bloodgroups of Aborigines supports the Out of Africa theory and Dreamtime stories, such as those from Arnhemland, which tell of ancestors coming from 'far across the sea'. Research on the rate of migration from Southern India to Australia about 65 k y a, puts the rate at four kilometres per year on average. Archaeologically, this 3,000 year journey is regarded as 'very rapid'.

In Flood's view, the ancient continent of Sahul which combined present day New Guinea, Australia and Tasmania, was probably inhabited (invaded) by humans 50-60 k y a when sea-levels were particularly low. At that time the Timor-Australia gap was only 70 km wide. In 1999 Robert Bednarik proved how the Timor crossing could be done using only stone-age tools and materials, in his Kontiki-type bamboo raft with palm-frond sails for the 13 day journey. Because of sea-level rise and northerly winds, the early migrants only had a one-way ticket, so the arrivals on Tiwi islands and others, became completely isolated.

Recent DNA studies suggest that the PNG migrations were between 40 and 70 k y a. Interestingly the oldest dated sites in northern Australia are inland, perhaps because there were few substantial caves on the coast. Flood reports that Polynesian and PNG adzes, with blades at right angles to handles, have not been found in Australia although the Dravidian (south Indian) backed-blades and points 'closely resemble' their Australian counter-parts. The woomera (spear thrower) appears to have spread South and West from Cape York, but never reached the NT islands of Bathhurst and Melville. So the NT islanders, isolated 6,500 years ago, fell short technologically. Similarly, isolated for 14,000 years, the Tasmanians exhibit big language differences from the mainland.

So Bro, say the migrants, get used to the idea that while you aren't a new-comer you are an old-comer in the sense that you did come from somewhere else. The good news is that while we're all migrants, we have always been human in the sense that we've always been *Homo sapiens*. So Australians have always been evolved beyond the 'sub-human' ancestors. This means that while the invaders of 1788 may have regarded the locals as 'primitive' by their standards and 'savage' by definition, they are basically the most modern evolutionary type.

In contemporary Australia there are over 90 national groups and Bro, you only make up 3%, which is less than several other groups such as Muslims or Greeks. You must never forget that there is great variation within your mob, which was there long before the whitefellas arrived and started mixing you even further. So It's good to remember that Mungo man was finer-boned, Kow Swamp man was courser-boned. One explanation is that the finer mob came from China and the courser mob from Java (Indonesia), at least according to Alan Thorne the anthropologist. Joseph Birdsell's theory, on the other hand, was that the ancestors arrived in three major waves: first the small and fine-boned mob of North Queensland which he called 'Barrineans', then there were the stocky solidly-built 'Murrayians' and after them were the taller 'Carpentarians'. It was this tall mob which most closely resembled the Southern Indians called 'Dravidians'.

Whatever the truth Bro, you are some kind of migrants who invaded the land of your totem animals, whom you killed for food. So you weren't here first, only the first upright mob.

THE STORY OF MY FIRST PEOPLES' INVASION AND DISPOSSESSION

My tribe is lucky to have our stories recorded in written form albeit decades after the devastating effects of invasion of our homeland. We'd been here for thousands of years, developing our own culture, belief system, language and social behaviour code.

As an indigenous nation we had our own religious leaders and tribal leaders and had developed a detailed knowledge of the plants and animals of our homeland. More importantly we were able to pass on knowledge to succeeding generations on how to live off the land, how to survive hard times and how to preserve our culture and traditions. All this came to an end when we were invaded by outsiders from over the sea. These newcomers had no right to claim our ancestral land and to kill those of our First People who resisted their takeover of our timeless landscape and all its spiritual connectedness to our people.

This story of oppression and enlightenment is recorded in a small leather-bound book dated MDCCLXXXIII, which is 333 years ago. Its titled 'An History of England in a series of Letters from a Nobleman to his Son', printed in St Paul's Churchyard, London, probably on a press very similar to Caxton's original.

Writing to his son Charles, the father uses the older English in which the letter 's' is written as 'f', giving some hilarious schoolboy howlers in pronunciation. He starts his third letter as follows:

'There seems to be a natural tendency in every nation to run its antiquity as far back as possible, and when they have arrived at the regions of fiction, no bounds are set to the wonder of every nation. Were we to take our character of the ancient inhabitants of this island from the legends, monuments or traditions, which have been left by those inhabitants themselves, we might be apt to imagine that arts, even in that early period, were cultivated, and services known in some degree of perfection. The Druids, if we believe some fragments of their own, understood astronomy and medicine, and gave lessons in morality and metaphysics. But what credit can be given to the accounts of a barbarous people, told by themselves? The knowledge and learning, indeed of their priests might be great, if compared with the almost brutal simplicity and ignorance of the rest of the people; but it could not deserve the name of science, if put in competition, with what was known and practised by their polite contemporaries of Greece and Rome.'

'From the accounts of those sensible writers, and not from the fictitious absurdities of the Druids themselves, we are to estimate this ancient people. The only motives of their choice were the peculiar fertility of some happy spot, or the convenience of wood and water. They lived upon milk and flesh, procured by the chase, for corn (wheat) was scarcely known among them. What clothes they wore were skins of beasts, but a great part of their bodies were left always exposed to the injuries of the weather...The custom of painting [their bodies] was universal among them. Their government, like that of the ancient Gauls (French) consisted of several petty principalities, which seem to be the original governments of mankind, deduced from the natural right of paternal dominion. Such were the customs of the ancient Britons, and the same may serve for a description of every other barbarous nation of which we have any knowledge. Savage man is an animal in almost every country the same; and all the difference between nations results from customs introduced by luxury, or cultivated by refinement. What the inhabitants of Britain was at that time, the inhabitants of South America or Kaffraria (South Africa) may be this day.'

'If the laity were so very barbarous, the Druids, their instructors, must have but few pretences to superior refinement. Their lives were simple and innocent, in woods, caverns and hollow trees, their food acorns or berries, and their drink water. The Druids, seeming formed for the people whom they governed, sacrificed human victims which they burned in large wicker idols, which were made so capacious, as to contain a multitude of persons, who were in this manner, consumed by the flames. The female Druids plunged their knives into the breasts of prisoners taken in war.'

'That the Druids deceived the people with a false religion cannot be denied, but yet I can never think that they were imposters. They first deceived themselves into a belief and veneration of what they taught and then they made use of every motive to persuade the people.'

'In short, the religion of the Druids was no more than that of every barbarous nation with whose ceremonies we have any acquaintance. Successive invasions from different ports of Asia brought new changes, and as the colonies went westward, the Greek, the Roman, and the Teutonic (Germanic) languages and customs were super-induced over the ancient Celtic. All the countries most accessible to strangers, or most subject to invasions, were first changed.'

[In letter IV, Charles' father continues]

'It is, in some measure, happy for a barbarous people to be conquered by a country more polite than themselves. Whatever evils the ambition of heroes generally produces, it is attended with one advantage, that of disseminating arts and making humanity more extensive. The Britons savage and rude as they were, in some measure called for more polite instructors; and the Romans, of all the conquerors history can produce, were at once the most polite, the most generous and humane.'

'A nation of herdsman and hunters can never be very populous; their subsistence takes up a large tract of country, while the husbandman converts every part of nature to human use, and produces the greatest quantity of subsistence from circumscribed possession.'

[In letter V, the writer describes the second Roman invasion of Britain by Claudius in 50 AD]:

'It is true that many Britons, who preferred their handy simplicity to imported elegance, rather than offer their necks to the Roman yoke, presented their breasts to the sword. But, by degrees, their fierceness was subdued or wholly destroyed...Here ended the liberties of Britain.'

'The Britons were also invaded by the Vikings, Saxons and Normans, all of whom had the effect of subduing the First Peoples' languages, religion, customs, ceremonies and laws. This overtaking of Indigenous traditions by more advanced peoples was repeated worldwide, until today the only Indigenous peoples remaining are those who preferred to maintain their original identity and 'natural' condition rather than adapt their lifestyle and identity to benefit from advanced well-being. Clearly many First Peoples have appreciated the education and health benefits of modernity while treasuring their historic tribal identity and the inner strength and sense of self which such a feeling of belonging conveys. But these forward-looking modernists have not allowed themselves to be defined by outdated cultural mores.'

It is hoped that the letters quoted here, give some perspective to our Aboriginal citizens, especially those who allow their lives to be permanently embittered by their inability to recognise that their on-going focus on 'colonial trauma', prevents them from enjoying the benefits brought by the newcomers to the ancient land.

Closer analysis indicates that time, the great healer, hasn't been sufficient to relegate this trauma to history. The fact that many of the disbenefits suffered from the unusually wide gap between the two cultures involved, are still alive in living memory, makes the Australian situation too fresh to be put in the ancient history category with the Briton's experience.

I trust this small window into British history allows Aborigines to recognise they are one of a large number of First Peoples whose 'primitive', earth-bound culture gave way to superior technologies and more refined values. This doesn't gainsay the value of traditional knowledge for past communities, but it gives substance to the truism that progress is accelerated by the influx of new ideas.

The message for Aboriginal leaders is: Keep history in its rightful place and don't let past dissatisfaction be confused with contemporary personal responsibility and initiative. Your present position may in fact not be all the government's fault. Recognise that while all the negative effects of dispossession are still deeply felt by the old people, the up-and-coming generation have the right to approach their modern challenges without having to shoulder residual, bitter baggage as insisted by many activists. What the young ones should be fighting for is contemporary justice and economic opportunity.

FROM THE SUBLIME TO THE RIDICULOUS: Mandela to Zuma, How the Law Moulded Them

This essay about reverse racism in the new South Africa, holds lessons for Australian Aborigines while this country prepares for its Recognition Referendum[3]. The lessons relate to the comparative equity which Aborigines enjoy, and the way in which the legislation of racism formed the basis of the Apartheid system. The material presented here should assist Indigenous Australians to view their present legal situation through the lens of Racial Relativism. This in turn, might encourage a more factual assessment of Australia's present human rights situation, despite the nation's poor historical record of the treatment of Aborigines.

A recent book 'Good Morning Mr Mandela' by Nelson Mandela's first secretary Zelda Le Grange is by any measure, a remarkable record of a remarkable man in remarkable times. As a personal account of a uniquely forgiving African president after 27 years in jail for opposing Apartheid, this book stands alone.

Many books have been written about Mandela's 'log cabin to Whitehouse' rise to President of the New South Africa. Without exception these accounts of political transition credit Mandela's big-hearted personality and inherent leadership qualities, with driving the eventual handover of power in 1994.

I came from the same region of South Africa as Mandela and my father sent our staff's son to boarding school in the same

---

[3] See note on page 210.

town as Mandela went to university to study law in the Eastern Cape Province. My university colleague and life-long friend, John Matthews, farmed at Alice and together we have watched the racial transition unfold. This was especially significant to the Matthews family when the Afrikaner government declared the area around the town of Alice to be a Black Homeland (named Ciskei under Apartheid) and the Matthews family had to abandon their generations-old farm when offered alternative land outside Ciskei.

Zelda's personal reflections on how Mandela's sheer strength of character and humanitarian values, changed her whole view of racism in South Africa, and are nothing less than a tear-jerking narrative. For those of us who wrestled with the morality of the system which had dominated our relations to our fellow citizens of other races in this human melting-pot at the southern tip of Africa, Zelda's writing cut deep.

Her story is especially poignant for those of us who lived with and understood the other side of the Afrikaner, the side which was formed by their own survival of two attempts to eliminate them as the only white indigenous people of Africa. Zelda's Afrikaans family were typical of that group who had, since 1652, evolved into a Christian land-based people, close to the earth and believing that they had been called by God to convert the dark people of the Dark Continent to the ways of their Lord. Biblical support for Apartheid was based on the passage that states the (dark) Sons of Hamm had been selected by God to forever be the hewers of wood and the carriers of water for the chosen people!

While such belief was later denounced by the very Dutch Reformed Church which claimed its holy truth, this recanting by the Church, was a long way off when Zelda's family brought up their children of the *Boerenasie*. Zelda's story is of particular significance today as it demonstrates firstly, that even the most ingrained racial stereotypes among the self-appointed 'superior' peoples can be changed, given mentors of integrity, and secondly, that the aspirations of multiculture's 'Rainbow Nation' can be dashed when iconic leadership is replaced by basic Africanism in its worst form.

What we now have in South Africa, is a tragedy of biblical proportions after unsurpassed humanitarian leadership had promised equality and non-racial constitutional rights to all. Under Apartheid since 1948, race classification and discrimination ruled the lives of both the privileged and the dispossessed. At Independence, the people were invited to vote in the first democratic election, for an end to racial discrimination. South Africa promised a meritocracy under a new Constitution which made it illegal to use racial background as a criterion for voting, employment, housing and organisational membership.

There was even a bold national attempt to cleanse the souls of the guilty by holding a macro-confession in the form of Bishop Tutu's 'Truth and Reconciliation Commission'. The idea was to wash away the sins of the perpetrators of past atrocities so that the emerging democracy could start with a clean sheet. Hindsight now tells us that while the largely religious sentiment of the TRC was to be applauded, the intensity and extent of the personal hurt caused by the vicious implementation of over 20 separate racial laws during a forty-year period, was never going to be erased or even softened by confessions of a few leaders of the most violent program of social engineering in modern times.

It is the depth of this hurt which made Mandela's forgiving spirit so remarkable, and for those of us who migrated because we foresaw a bloody end to Apartheid, Mandela's forgiveness was surprising and almost surreal. It is for precisely this reason that

Zelda's experiences and eventual enlightenment are potentially so cathartic to those Whites whose racialism was indoctrinated into them from an early age. The fashionable phrase is 'it's in our DNA'. But it isn't and that's the point of Zelda's conversion and how it spilled over to her conservative family and friends.

To help outsiders understand the extent of the legal framework which supported Apartheid, a concise history of how legislation had excluded Blacks since the earliest days of colonisation, forms a useful background to modern White racism.

Those who grew up under Apartheid, recognise that racism was alive and well long before 1948. Since federation of the four provinces into the Union of South Africa in 1910, racism has been reflected in the country's early legislation. By the time my parents married in the early 1930's, the country already had several racially-based acts on the books: The South Africa Act (1910); The Native Lands Act (1913); the Native Urban Areas Act (1915); and the Immorality Act (1927). Space does not allow for description of the impacts of each Act listed here, on the Black populations, nor is the intent of each Act clear from its title. However the reader can assume that in combination, all these legal constraints were aimed at:

i.   Keeping the races separate socially.
ii. Facilitating a permanent supply of very cheap labour for industry and domestic need.
iii. Preventing the organisation of political opposition.

The focus of today's Generation X in South Africa, is to achieve precisely the opposite of the above aims.

When my wife and I married in 1956 a series of new Acts had

been passed to a legal framework for the all-encompassing Apartheid policy. These included the Representation of Natives Act (1936); the Native Laws Act (1937); the Black Urban Areas Act (1945); the Prohibition of Mixed Marriages Act (1949); the Population Registration Act (1950); the Suppression of Communism Act (1950); the Suppression of Terrorism Act (1951); the Reservation of Separate Amenities Act (1953); the Resettlement of Natives Act (1954) and the Separate Representation of Voters Act (1956).

During the years that we were bringing up our children, more desperate legal protection of white privilege was enacted: the Unlawful Organisations Act (1960); the General Law Act (1964); the Terrorism Act (1967); the Prohibition of Political Interference Act (1968) and the Internal Security Act (1982).

These lists don't include the early Mines and Works Act (1911) which prevented Natives from undergoing training for skilled employment, or the wide-ranging Group Areas Act passed in the year I left school (1950). Nor do the lists include the strangely-titled Abolition of Passes and Co-ordination of Documents Act (1952) which actually imposed further pass laws rather than abolishing them. These passes refer to the hated Bantu Pass Books, the identification documents which Blacks had to carry at all times. The above catalogue of legislation is detailed here so that Australian Aborigines can appreciate their relative position.

During the 1980's both internal and external opposition to Apartheid increased to the point where, by the parliamentary session of January 1986, President Botha had little option but to declare Apartheid 'an outdated concept'. That was the easy part; the difficult part was convincing his compatriots that the game was up on White supremacy. Forty years of both privilege and pain had officially come to an end.

Perhaps outsiders find it difficult to imagine how deeply this regime-change affected the Afrikaner descendants of those who fought in the Zulu and Boer Wars. Nor were the English-speaking Whites immune to the coming reversal of roles in the master/servant relations which they had enjoyed for many generations. This need for adaptation to the new deal, forms the burden of Zelda's story, a story which started so well but was to lead to unspeakable levels of corruption, tribalism and lawless activity which followed Mandela's retirement, first during Thabo Mbeki's presidency, then reaching heights unseen in modern times, during Jacob Zuma's rule.

The shift from the sublime to the ridiculous in political leadership must surely be one of the greatest declines in governance integrity in world history, especially since this disaster has occurred in under two decades. The difference between the Mandela aspirations and the Zuma crisis, is much more exaggerated than in other African countries for two prime reasons:

i.   The competing races both represented a history of intense pride and persistence in the face of armed aggression.

ii.   The South African industrialised economy, built originally on British expertise, offered greater opportunities for looting of well-financed entities, than anywhere else in Africa, where subsistence economies typified their Third World status.

Meanwhile White South Africans, Indians and Coloureds currently have several options:

i.   They can maintain their identity and use their shrewd

47

business acumen to run their small business at a profit even under discriminatory regulations which favour Africans,

ii.   They can join the Black power-brokers and denounce their racial inheritance in favour of patronage by the Zulu-led government, as many of them have; or

iii. They can emigrate to other English-speaking countries where Hindu and Christian communities of their people are already well established.

And the Afrikaners? Presently their rural land ownership is threatened by legalised takeover by the government. I know many who are 'hanging in there', but I know even more Afrikaners who see migration as their only long-term hope. The Rainbow Nation which they voted for has disappeared.

Aboriginal Australians are invited to compare their situation with the very different South African position, when considering their forthcoming constitutional recognition.

WHO STOLE OUR RAINBOW?
South Africa Today and Lessons for Aboriginal Traditionalists

Comparative racism always helps to develop a clearer assessment of one's own particular situation. In this case, the recent South African experience of racism by Blacks, offers insightful comparisons from which Australian Aboriginals and their government can learn.

When Apartheid ended in 1994 and Mandela envisioned his Rainbow Nation, his spirit of forgiveness and hope for a non-racial future came as a great relief. Forty-six years of enforced separation and discrimination miraculously came to a bloodless end, much to the surprise of migrants such as myself, who had decided to remove my family from the madness in 1975.

Realistically, nobody was surprised by the way the new Black government worked urgently to right past wrongs by appointing their own people to positions of power at all the levels of government, irrespective of expertise and experience. Nor did the citizens of the New South Africa expect the African National Congress (ANC) to operate a Westminster-type merit-based democracy with so much lost time to make up for. Squaring the ledger and pay-back time had arrived.

What they didn't foresee was the way in which old-fashioned tribalism would not just influence the ANC in its nation-wide appointments, but would totally dominate the way the ANC did business. Today 'tribalism' is a dirty word despite the fact that it is clearly recognised as the driver of present power-plays.

Most informed observers, notably those Whites who still had families in South Africa, suspected that the magnanimity of Mandela was not only unusual and globally admired, but was unlikely to last when the dog-eat-dog realities of tribal rivalries were brought to bear on local politics.

Expecting forgiveness by the long-oppressed majority to lead on to a happy ending in which real equality and Samaritanism ruled, was always going to be something of a vain hope. Archbishop Tutu's Truth and Reconciliation Commission (TRC) which sought reconciliation between the perpetrators and victims of Apartheid atrocities, was to be a catharsis allowing a new start. This bold attempt to put the past behind us, was heavily religious in its attempt to rid South Africa of its sins and achieve an elusive forgiveness for half a century of evil. The TRC was a unique national confession, unprecedented in racial history and led to a score of publications, most of which were theologically based. The reason for such religiosity was not hard to find. Firstly, the Dutch Reformed Church (DRC) which anchored the Afrikaner people had for decades insisted that Apartheid was biblically anointed and that separatism was the will of God. Secondly, the oppressed Blacks, especially their women, had long sought comfort from their mission-based Christian faith as their only safe harbour in the family-destroying storm of discriminatory laws which are listed in the previous essay.

While Mandela was being given well-earned royal treatment internationally, the ANC machine-men were already carving up the spoils of democracy. Soon it became clear that public service came a poor second to the get-rich-quick syndrome which set in at an alarming rate. Tribal rivalries added a cut-throat edge to the dispensations of patronage, powerful positions and government tenders.

At the time of Independence (1994) the country recognised 13 official languages representing as many tribal entities. By 2010, the ANC had reduced its list of recognised tribes (officially 'ethnic entities') to two – Zulus and Xhosas. The others still existed but carried no political clout.

Today South Africa is suffering from the paralysing effects of a democracy gone wrong. In my report of 2010 entitled 'South Africa Revisited: A Migrant looks Back and Forward,' I recorded how many of my old friends were disappointed in my assessment of the New South Africa as a 'failed state'. This assessment was based on the criteria of:

i.   The rule of law.
ii.   Equality of opportunity.
iii.   Freedom of the press.
iv.   Productivity as reflected in the employment rate.

With the benefit of hindsight, it is informative to now bring in the writings of R.W. Johnson, an Oxford don, with a remarkably detailed knowledge of South African politics. Johnson, a South African white, had long supported the ANC and the anti-apartheid cause. So much so that in 1977 he wrote 'How Long Will South Africa Survive?' an in-depth analysis of the failure of Apartheid. In 2015 he produced a second volume under the same title but adding the subtitle: 'The Looming Crisis'. This recent work unpacks Johnson's disillusionment with the ANC and its total incapacity to apply the fundamentals of a functioning democracy. In his words: 'I decided that the most valuable thing I could do was to chronicle this unparalleled experiment in which Third World nationalism came to power in a (relatively) developed country. Nothing like this had ever happened before.'

Johnson's exposé follows the compilation edited by Peter Vale *et al* titled 'Intellectual Traditions in South Africa', published by my Alma Mater the University of Kwazulu-Natal. Readers of Vale would be forgiven for wondering whether the chapter authors were requested to avoid criticism of the present government and the ANC in these collected essays. With the exception of Helen Moffett on Feminism, who lays into male macho behaviour, the other authors seem content to limit their comments to intellectual apolitical matters while Rome burns.

If raw tribalism, strong-man tactics, corruption and the failure of the legal system concerns these academics, it is hard to detect in the writings presented. Vale insists that this compilation, 'Is the beginning of a conversation about South Africanness that is long, long overdue'. He is correct, but even more overdue and far more urgent, is the need for intellectuals to have the courage and commitment to say it as it is, in the obvious collapse of democracy. I'd invite all these intellectuals to read Johnson's (2012) 'The African University: The Critical Case of South Africa and the Tragedy of UKZN (University of Kwa Zulu – Natal).' Their comment could be compiled into a second volume which should make a real contribution to the contemporary non-debate about how and why the state is failing.

Allied to the above debate on how the ANC is encouraging tribalism, is a third recent publication titled 'The Colour of our Future: Does Race Matter in Post-Apartheid South Africa'. This is a welcome comparison of views on how the non-racial ideals of the new Constitution are being negated by the insidious re-intro-duction of a different racism to the old Apartheid black/white type. Post racial South Africa is rapidly being lost to an ANC-fuelled tribal racism whose 'I'm proud to be Black' mantra contradicts the 'I don't see race' concept of the conciliators. In the process of encouraging Black Pride, the hopes of Steve Biko's 'Joint Cultures' are taking a back seat. This volume does much to argue the case that race is being replaced by class as a self-identifier. However, the old clan loyalties of Zulus, Xhosas and Indians remain powerful forces in today's society. Black Consciousness is increasing ethnic pride now that black means power.

The Chapter by Lawrence Blum (U, Mass., US) compares racial identity in South Africa and America, starting with Johann Blumenbach's late 1700s five-class racial grouping: Malayan, Ethiopian (African), American, Caucasian and Mongoloid. This generalised grouping has stood the test of time but has been undermined by the scientific rejection of any biological basis for race identification. Blumenbach's five races were believed to exhibit seven recognisable features which could be used as reliable criteria of distinction. Today it is recognised that these racial groups do not, in fact, possess these seven characteristics. The social reality of racialisation however, is such that irrespective of science, in practice people do distinguish between others who appear different.

Why does this theory matter? Because South Africa, with its new non-racial Constitution is now governed by a new ANC ideology which does emphasise 'ethnic groups' and their clear distinction. While President Zuma pays lip-service to non-racialism his many actions through tribal appointments to powerful positions and his non-action against the looting of the public purse, speaks volumes for his Zulu patriotism. The result of this approved self-serving tribalism has spawned a Zulu elite who have taken over both government contracts and local government. In the process, public funding of utilities has been cleaned out to the extent that the citizens have established their own service organisations in the municipal, police and education spheres because government is failing them.

The obvious question to ask is 'How does the democratic process allow this to happen? The answer is that in the crudest of Third World power-plays, the ANC has managed to pull the wool over voter's eyes in their orchestrated campaign to sing the praises of the Zuma team. However, as an earlier US president observed: You can fool all the people some of the time and some of the people all the time, but you cannot fool all the people all the time.

At this juncture it is instructive to consider the emerging role of an increasingly educated constituency and their understanding of their democratic rights under the Constitution. Just as the Afrikaners had developed politically-oriented universities at Stellenbosch, Bloemfontein, Pretoria and Potchefstroom in an effort to bolster the cause of Afrikaner nationalism, so the ANC has taken over most of the present universities. Black Vice Chancellors now abound and senior appointments are made within the ambit of 'Affirmative Action' based on preferential treatment of Black applicants.

Under this policy my former employer the University of the Free State which started as an English-speaking college and became an Afrikaans university under the Apartheid government, is now scheduled to revert to English as the language of Instruction in 2017. The Universities of Cape Town and Witwatersrand, the two most liberal seats of higher learning continue to fight the good fight against politicisation, as they always have, but the others have already lost their souls as serious contenders for international respect as genuinely 'open'. African Nationalism comes at a high price in tertiary education even if standards are maintained, which they aren't in several cases. The price is international competitiveness of graduates and the critical brain-drain of senior profession-als to meritocracies elsewhere.

Government demands for high pass rates through 'affirmative marking' (!) will see the chickens come home to roost as the next generation become managers and captains of industry.

What has made many of the most productive citizens, both White and Black, leave South Africa in the past decade, is the breakdown of law enforcement. In contrast to the well-worded Constitution, the manner in which the police force and the judicial system generally function are at the heart of the failing state. This is evident in both the lack of prosecutions for crimes against individuals and the extraordinary failure of legal action against high-ranking officials, from the President down. Zuma himself allegedly has over 700 charges against him, mostly for fraud. Treating the public purse as a family bank account has apparently become a widespread phenomenon. When many millions of dollars allocated for Mandela's funeral went missing and when the driver of a murder get-away car was found to be a policeman, the voters realised that the rot had set in.

The outside observer can only conclude that South Africa's salvation must come by way of an internal revolt within the ANC. Change cannot come from pressure applied by Opposition parties under present circumstances. This is simply because of the extent patronage, alleged bribery and corruption increasingly have sidelined any significant political threat from other parties. The revolt will probably be led by the poverty-stricken masses of ANC members whose disdain for present political fat-cats is apparently fast reaching breaking point.

As with the demise of Apartheid, so the privileged elite of the ANC have the choice of changing direction or having it changed for them by the majority. So while the privileged bling class could experience their own Bastille day, many like to believe that the more likely scenario is the recognition by the ANC that the game is up for the tribalists. Those in power will hopefully acknowledge that their well-worded Constitution must indeed set the rules of engagement, in which polygamist tribal chiefdoms have no place.

While South Africa's second miraculous peaceful transition attracts us optimists, Mother Africa has repeatedly shown herself to still be prone to tribal patriotism being put ahead of national cohesion. Having achieved the old 'Africa for the Africans' post-colonial objective, tribal warfare has shown itself to be just below the surface, even in these modern times. Zuma's 'democracy' exists under the thinnest of civilised veneers and while all would hope for a social democratic handover of political power, it would be naive to assume the reality of such civility. Much as I would hope for the Westminster system of government to prevail, as a descendant of a frontier settler, I'd instinctively be inclined to keep my powder dry.

Australian Aborigines who are keen to maintain tribal identity and tradition, would do well to consider the lessons of separatism and clan loyalty learned from South Africa. Resilience, adaptation, tolerance and participation in the mainstream, is where the best future lies.

PART TWO
Aboriginality

DIVERSITY AND UNITY:
We Are One But We Are Many

It is always infuriating for a writer, when a superior wordsmith pips you at the post, on an idea that you've been trying to articulate for yonks. This happened to me when Brendon O'Neill of The Australian (7/8/15) wrote: 'Today's sanctification of diversity is really an assault on unity.' He was referring to the schizophrenia which many Australians probably feel when the 'Who are we?' question comes up, as it increasingly does in these times of uncertainty.

Our national anthem highlights our diverse backgrounds, and the way we pride ourselves on welcoming those of other faiths, customs and languages into the bosom of our community. Recently however, the threat of terrorism has made us pause and ask: 'Have we been too welcoming, too trusting and even too naive about the realities of radicalised religious bigots'? Several incidents, notably at schools, churches and shopping centres, have made us wake up from our cultural slumber and start asking ourselves whether we actually value our own cultural inheritance.

O'Neill is only one of the commentariat who has said what many are thinking, and has asked questions which most of us were afraid to ask. Some years ago, before Islamic terrorism was the home-grown threat it is today, religious leaders, charities and independent politicians started asking whether we were (unconsciously?) excluding our Muslim citizens in the way we acted in public or in groups. Then conflict began with Christmas Carols being seen by our over-sensitive colleagues as performances which did nothing for the sense of belonging of some of our immigrants. Then it was Nativity displays in shop windows and supermarkets which were seen as alienating non-Christians. This was followed by questioning when and where the national anthem should be sung; an activity which most in the mainstream would support and encourage. In November 2015 it all came to a head when it was dubbed 'Anthem gate' by the press. The ruckus started when Muslim students were granted permission to leave school assembly when 'Australia Fair' was being sung by students and staff. On enquiry, it turned out that the Muslim cleric of the region had stated that forcing students to sing the anthem was a form of forced assimilation. Kids should not be obliged to participate in customs which reflect historical views which are in conflict with their family's beliefs, seemed to be his message.

In the usual style of sub-editing of The Australian, the caption 'Singing from the same songbook...' seemed pointed enough in political terms. Our leaders repeatedly encourage us all to sing from the same hymn sheet, but the caption's reference to 'disciples of difference' would have touched a nerve in many in our Islamic community. Many might ask whether this applies equally to Indigenous separatists and Christian fundamentalists.

Perhaps Australia is becoming stuck in the bog of group identity and belonging. Thus while we're assured our commonality far outweighs our differences as cultural groups, the role of Left and Right thinking in the integration/separation debate, is more than a little confused. The Left is often accused of overemphasising differences and thus it is blamed for dividing the populace in its insistence that each culture/language/religion be valued and respected in and of itself. The Right conservatives are seen as retreating into their historic cultural fortress in an attempt to escape the discomfort of having to live with the awkward 'multi' element of our cultural soup. The much-vaunted 'Australian way of life' also comes in for a shellacking by the religious purists, who see our behaviours as far from moral and as such, nowhere near providing a good model for our offspring.

In essence we have a series of identity issues: The first is the lack of agreement on what mainstream Australia's core values actually are. The second is the extent to which we should expect migrants to integrate into our behaviour/values construct. The third is the potential for mainstream Australia to actually appreciate and adopt values of tolerance, integrity and religious grounding which some of our new chums can offer.

If the Left is dividing us, what is the Right doing? There is confusion on national objectives here, and it is this split personality of the Australian which leads us to attempt to amalgamate the splitters and lumpers. In Aboriginal terms, we have a very different unity problem based on past wrongs. With our migrants we start with a positive balance: you're wanting to leave your homeland; we are happy to welcome you into our capitalist democracy; we hope you'll integrate into our society but we also value your cultural diversity. The Aboriginal position is very different. The mainstream admits to taking over their country, but insists that it's for their own good. Aboriginal separatism is different from Muslim separatism, but the essential element of integration without loss of identity remains a major issue for both minority groups. Adding to complexities is a lack of respect for Aborigines by the Muslims who share none of the inferred Whitefella guilt of past wrongs.

Many observers have posed the question of the difference

between rich diversity and unproductive divisiveness. Both Muslims and Aborigines accuse the mainstream of side-lining them, of isolating them from the economic and political mechanisms of the nation. The reasons for this sense of being a nobody in the world's most successful multiculture, are not only difficult to validate, but seem almost impossible to gain agreement on. The fact that personal isolation is given as the prime reason for home-grown terrorists emerging from otherwise peaceful Islamic communities, has of course focussed recent attention on Muslims. The Aborigines, like the Republic or the Flag or the Anthem, often seem to be regarded as a non-urgent issue – a view vastly different from that of Aboriginal spokespersons who have grown weary in their long-standing campaign to reduce incarceration rates, to improve employment and health, and to finally gain acceptance as valued citizens through first class education. Their increasing demand for various rights, including land, has recently led to accusations of the government not listening.

There remain at least two fundamental problems for our not-very-well disguised social engineers:

i. Identifying whose fault it is, that groups who feel marginalised, have difficulty in integrating.
ii. Determining how best to motivate groups who feel marginalised/isolated/vilified/unwanted, into joining the mainstream.

Before attempting to solve these problems, it is worth recognising that many on the Left don't seem to see any merit in social cohesion and its common vision. In fact these separatists see unity as a pale alternative to their relativist model in which all cultures are valued equally, are equally worth preserving as distinct 'Australian' subcultures, and are far preferable to the colourless and culture-free mishmash of many mixed cultures elsewhere.

All those groups looking for public comments to prove that theirs is an oppressed minority of victims and martyrs, can always find some oddball out of left field, making statements which fuel their conspiracy theory. Many of the contemporary claims of racism, originate from these activists who are ever on the lookout for racist ammunition. Both Muslims and Aboriginals have activists who specialise in what I have elsewhere called 'the emerging art of offense-taking'. It has become clear that there can be no complete elimination of such racist claims in a country which prides itself on free speech and operates under both the Defamation Act and the Racial Discrimination Act.

When PM Turnbull gave one of his long explanations of the dangers of Islamophobia his punch line was: 'the one thing we really need is respect.' Personally, I thought 'tolerance' would have been more fitting.

WE JUST WANT
TO BE OURSELVES

David Ross of the Central Land Council in Alice Springs wrote a great introduction to Mary Bowman's book 'Every Hill Got a Story' (August 2015). The story covers all facets of the history of the Indigenous Centralians, from the life of the desert myalls, through white contact, the influence of missionaries, life on reserves under the Protector, massacres by pastoralists and their agents, and finally Native Title and Ross's people's efforts toward self-management.

It is surprising that no reviewer seems to have taken Ross up on his insistence that his people should be allowed to 'be who we are'. He asks the authorities to stop trying to change them into 'someone else'. It is at this point that Ross's great story should be carefully analysed.

Lets agree that serious policy mistakes were made in the past and that Indigenous people have suffered as a result. The trauma of dispossession still affects the older generations and needs to be accounted for in contemporary policy, to aid positive transition to present society and well-being. At the same time we should take Pearson's 2007 advice and 'be done once and for all with (white) guilt and shame over past discriminatory policies...'. This is not easily done but should offer a challenging aspiration for us all.

Against this conciliatory background, let us consider the implications of 'being who we are'. This statement is of central importance in the present 'recognition' debate and it presupposes not only that we know who we are, but that we also know what we want our offspring to be. Clarity on this matter is of particular significance for those champions of Indigenous identity. Personal identity is meaningless if it is value free. If for instance, a friend of mine says, 'I'm a proud Kamillaroy man', we need to understand where that pride is founded. Is it founded simply on inherited family ties and beliefs, or is it founded on a sense of values which stand up to modern humanitarian scrutiny?

I have elsewhere listed the useful catalogue of human qualities proposed by Prof. Ken Wiltshire of the University of Queensland, as a basis for our education system. It is expressed as a series of statements which answer the questions:

- We aim to develop future citizens who stand for ...
- and who value ...
- and who act in such a way as to ...

While this list is a mainstream construction and may not agree with Indigenous values, it behoves Indigenous leaders to come up with clear elucidation of what 'being ourselves' actually implies. But more than that, it encourages Indigenous leaders to gain consensus among their people on the extent to which they're ready to appreciate their children's future and the modern realities which that brings.

Ross is probably not saying we can't adapt or change, or leave some elements of our historic traditions in the past. He's probably saying we really do want to run our own show. We want to progress and adopt better ways in our own way and in our own time. He is sufficiently educated and articulate to make a telling case for his people, but he will need to persuade the less empathetic mainstream that while history is both interesting and important in understanding his people's contemporary situation, it is not sufficient to guide future policy directions. Ross and his fellow Centralians like Rosalie Kunoth Monks and Tracker Tilmouth and others, vary somewhat in their emphasis on the extent to which tribal identity defines them. More importantly, they also differ in their estimation of the benefits of joining the mainstream and the extent to which this constitutes cultural genocide.

Ross's view of the future is probably not as clear as his unusually well-informed view of the past. This applies to most of us no doubt, but if Indigenous leaders are to seriously benefit their coming generations, who are the hope of their people's future, they will need to be somewhat less 'precious' about traditional matters and insistence on the never-changing edicts of their law.

It is precisely this personal judgement of the extent to which our tribal identity is allowed to define our values, behaviour and relationships with outsiders, which forms the crux of our inclusion in the nation. Migrants of all cultures and religions have this personal decision to make – and it is our decision, nobody else's.

However, inclusion has two sides to it: our readiness to accept others and others' willingness to accept us. Many migrants, including myself, have been deeply hurt by being stereotyped on the basis of our people's history. Others have been hurt by being shunned or ignored, apparently because of their appearance, their accent or their faulty speech. There seems to be a fear of 'the other' as different, alien, untrustworthy or even threatening. Being different has its costs for all of us. [I can remember my African associates telling me that Whites smell different, a sour smell.]

So David Ross has to decide that the 'us' he wants to be, is an 'us' who are willing to modify, to change, to adapt, to acknowledge, to tolerate, to live and let live. My guess is that he'd do this better than many mainstreamers. But the acid test will come when he sees their reaction to his willingness to be inclusive. Ross has of course been dealing with whitefellas all his life, but the new deal of being ourselves, offers a new and level playing-field in which we can be ourselves on our terms, and our terms include our being acceptable and inclusive to our increasingly welcoming new chums.

We must all take the risk and extend the hand of friendship. The new Australian way.

ABSOLUTELY ABORIGINAL:
The Search for Author Authenticity

I have spent many years studying Aboriginal history and policy. Having grown up with tribal children in Africa, I believe I may be able to put myself in their shoes. On the strength of this empathy, I wrote a book titled 'Jean's Story', set in North Queensland. Despite careful avoidance of a negative or demeaning portrayal of the Aboriginal characters in my narrative, I have copped considerable vitriolic criticism for presuming to speak for 'the Other': How dare you. What arrogance. You've never lived among Aborigines. You stereotype us. You have no right. You show no respect. You can never be authentic. What would a migrant know? Could an ex-South African ever understand? And on it goes.

While I was contemplating my capitulation or defence, a friend sent me a little-known research paper by Linda Miley, which delved deeply into precisely this question of who can speak for whom. 'Jean's Story' doesn't emerge completely unscathed from Miley's incisive academic analysis of non-Indigenous (aka white) authors who enter the murky waters of Aboriginality. I take some comfort from Langton's (1993) more advanced view of the potential value of white authors to Aboriginal understanding and well-being.

Unsurprisingly, the contemporary, more sympathetic and diplomatic writers on Aboriginal matters, such as Fred Cheyney, Jeff McMullen, Nicolas Rothwell and various church spokespersons, seldom raise the ire of the blackfellas. Juxtaposed to these fellow-travellers are those Aboriginal writers who suggest that neither sympathy nor respect can be expected from the mainstream, until simple norms of individual responsibility are met by the complainants.

Back in 1958, Katherine Susannah Pritchard got away with 'Coonardo's' mixed love affair, and in 1972 Thomas Keneally's 'The Chant of Jimmie Blacksmith' succeeded in winning hearts for the half-cast Jimmie when he intruded into white womanhood. In the interim a culture of offensive racism has arisen.

Langton is correct when she points out that white authors who 'homogenise' Aborigines as a non-differentiated mob, misrepresent the reality of Aboriginality. It is for this reason that Jean's Story portrays three Aboriginal students as a bushy, a fringe-dweller and a city-slicker. The narrative goes on to contrast the Pearsons of Hopevale with the Yunupingus of Arnhemland.

Moreton-Robinson, in 'Whitening Race' (2004) points out how white writers have presented Aborigines in negative terms since colonial times, eg. childish, primitive, savage, treacherous, cunning and dirty. Others have recognised a nobility, a spirituality and a sacred respect for ancestors and nature, although their religious attributes were invariably judged by outsiders to be inferior to those of advanced white culture.

Miley, in her 'Leaning Into The Light' thesis (2006), fairly asks: 'How does the white author write on 'other' people, whose entire cultural history has been erased (by invaders)?' She partially answers her own question by citing both Langton and Janke, as Aboriginal critics, who see fruitful and creative writing emanating from white writers who appreciate ethical protocols as part of author recognition. In my narration of 'Jean's Story', reviewers have remarked on the Aboriginal characters' language being too mainstream and their worldliness being beyond expectations. Such criticism reflects on my positive attempt to not downplay the potential of educated, young Aborigines to become both articulate and humanitarian in a global sense.

This whole concept of authenticity falls apart when it is shown to be incapable of handling the difference between being a 'real' Aborigine and being both logical and reasonable. My approaches to two Indigenous publishers were knocked back because I was not a recognised member of an Aboriginal community. Neither publisher wanted to know whether my narrative was supportive of Aboriginal self-determination or whether my writings respected Aboriginal culture. Neither were interested in the case I was making for encouraging young Aboriginal professionals to serve their own mob, to ease the plight of their old folks, or to encourage higher norms in education and personal responsibility.

I understand the goals of these publishers to offer publishing opportunities to their own people, but they seem unaware of the way they are selling their people short on outside help, outside drive and outside political influence. As Gray so well described the bind of the supportive non-Indigenous writer in 2000: 'For those non-Indigenous writers willing to risk the perils of writing on Aboriginal themes and characters, there is a double bind, i.e. if they're positive and supportive, the writer risks accusations of 'whitewashing' the real situation for their middle-class readership.' If the writer is negative, there will be accusations of what Gray terms 'ghettoising' of Aborigines and reinforcing the view that 'they can't be trusted to take personal responsibility'. This inescapable risk may lead Australian authors to give issues of Aboriginality a wide berth and this, in Wheatly's (1997) view, holds the real danger of our literature presenting a white Australian monoculture as a result of excluding 'the other'.

This narrowing of views and tolerances led Langton (1993) to make the case for white writers with experience of Aborigines, to be given the space to contribute by way of what she called 'inter-subjectivity' – a cross-cultural, inward-looking capacity to appreciate realities and shortcomings on both sides. Ethical critique by white writers is achievable in Langton's view. She challenges the assumption that 'Aboriginal people are able to make 'better' representations of being Aboriginal' (Miley 2006). Langton maintains that such an assumption is based on acceptance of 'otherness', regardless of individual variations. Miley suggests that while Indigenous protocols can provide 'culturally sensitive directives' for white writers, these don't necessarily lead to the 'best outcomes' – meaning valid assessment of Aboriginal values and behaviour.

A case in point is that of Phillip Gwynne, a white author whose novel 'Deadly Unna' was converted to the film 'Australian Rules'. When criticised for taking it upon himself to characterise the Aborigine in the story, Gwynne said, 'It's a white story which intersects 100% with black people's lives.' He denied anyone the right to prevent him telling his story, founded on a real event in his life.

Writer's Protocols

When writing 'Jean's Story', which is a positive narrative about transitioning young Aboriginal post-graduates, I was well aware of cultural correctness and its implications. So, when confronted with the writings of an Aboriginal legal advisor, such as Terri Janke, the significance of authenticity loomed large. Like Gwynne, I saw my writing as my story, which needed no further authenticity than my experience with students of all shades over fifty years, nor were my black childhood friends forgotten.

Predictably, having someone like Janke reflect on my credentials, would cause a defensive reaction. So I was glad to read that writers like Miley, well versed in appropriateness, suggest that the need for Janke's type of authenticity is debatable, at least academically (which I take to mean rationally). Authenticity is held up as a means of gaining Indigenous co-operation and respect. Janke (2003) maintains that authenticity refers to the 'cultural source of Indigenous material, so proper consideration of authenticity shows respect for customary laws or cultural obligations…' This, says Janke, ensures engagement with the owners of the material. Maybe this idea relates more to art and artefacts, than to writing, and it should be noted that protocols aren't legally binding anyway.

In the case of narratives, Wheatley (1997) says white writers writing Aboriginal characters should give thought to 'respect and politeness' and Miley agrees that sensitivities of this type should be paramount for white writers. This sensitive, non-critical, culturally appropriate requirement presents a serious reality problem for the Aboriginal community. It relates to truth, validity and wishful thinking and it has recently come into sharp focus as a result of a few enlightened 'authentic' Aboriginal spokespersons telling it as it is. Not only are these honest critics of their own mob branded as Coconuts (white inside) or Turncoats, but they are attacked for letting the team down. The opposite is of course true, because they're not only authentic (as measured by the unwritten rules of authenticity), but they bring a breath of fresh air to the closed-shop of fabricated correctness.

This schism in the ranks resembles the effect of the Renaissance on the Dark Ages, but there are no referees, no ultimate judges, to award the case to the Enlightened. Experienced scholars of Aboriginal policy, hold that the fundamental problem is the absence of agreed goals and aspirations for this highly diversified mob of differentiated individuals. And it is this lack of a common vision which continues to allow the uncompetitive traditionalists to preach cultural genocide as the label for progress. In the sphere of white writers attempting to bring mature depiction of all facets of black/white relations, the dead hand of offence-taking under the guise of defending precious culture, has long since seen good supporters leave the contest of ideas for adult debate elsewhere.

We write about Jews, Arabs, Africans, Asians, Indians, Chinese and English. No other people demand Indigenous DNA as a qualification for writing about them, so why is traditional blood so important here? The truthful answer is that a lack of competitiveness has caused the traditionalists to retreat into the refuge of concocted authenticity.

Most white authors don't write for Aborigines but write about Aborigines, as perceived through what Bradshaw (2001) saw as filtering Aboriginality through a white perspective. The question arises as to whether this filtered product is more insightful or useful than the alternative. The other question of who speaks for whom, has become the puerile plaything of hyper-sensitive academics who themselves are unable to define authenticity in any meaning-ful way. Part of the Ivory Tower talk-fest is the deep question of 'the other'. Is it good to be 'other'? How's it defined? What does it stand for? Who thinks it's a good idea to belong? Are there policy benefits? In academe, there is serious conflict about what charac-terises 'the other'. The original 'other people' seem to be character-ised by being:

i.   Very ancient.

ii. Lack a civil history.

iii. Unchanging and thus unadaptable.

iv. Have an all-pervasive natural spirituality.

v.   Use 'primitive' gender roles.

vi. Regard change as detrimental to culture and thus to identity.

Assuming that there is also a modern 'other', it seems to be characterised by:

i.   Strong family ties.

ii.   Obligations to share with kinfolk.

iii. Pride in achievement.

iv.   Potentially high sporting prowess.

v.   Determination to overcome discrimination.

vi.   Demand human rights.

vii. Demand respect.

viii. Value education.

Various academic dissertations describe the concept of 'other' as mysterious, exotic, erotic, timeless and somehow precious, mainly because of what it is not, i.e. how it differs from the faulty alternatives of a greedy, selfish, egotistic and materialistic invader culture which is reflected in the worst aspects of colonialism, capitalism, and modernity.

While the mainstream assessment of what is 'un-Australian' will probably remain a dynamic concept as social values change, the question of what is 'un-Aboriginal', probably produces an even wider continuum of opinions. Meanwhile debates rage on authenticity, otherness and who may speak for whom. Currently Langton's idea of Inter-subjectivity as the fundamental element of representation, is probably the most useful approach available.

Literature on Aboriginality

Miley (2006) has produced one of the more informative searches on race literature and portrayal of blacks by whites. She uses overseas publications to reinforce Australian positions, starting with 'Black Looks: Race And Representation' (US 1992) by b. cooks (distinguished by his use of lower case proper nouns). This is augmented by Brown and Sant's 'Indigeneity: Construction and Re-presentation' (US 1999) and T. Goldie's 'The Representation of the Indigene' in The Post Colonial Reader (UK 1995).

I have given a comprehensive review of racial literature elsewhere (Race, Colour and Opportunity in *Quadrant Online*, Brian Roberts 13/05/14). In summary, it seems obvious that if Aboriginal Literature is to be taken seriously at international level, the 'unauthentic' writers will need to be welcomed into the debate before Aboriginal recognition can be expected.

THE ABORIGINAL INDUSTRY REVISITED

Back in the 1990's Deputy Prime Minister, Tim Fischer used to travel his rural constituency warning his flock of the emerging Aboriginal Industry; a coalescence of activists intent on promoting Aboriginal cultural primacy as a basis for policy formulation in Indigenous Affairs. By the end of 2013 Frances Widdowson and Albert Howard published their stirring Canadian book titled: 'Disrobing the Aboriginal Industry: The deception behind Indigenous Cultural Preservation'.

When assessing Widdowson's view that the Indigenous cultural/spiritual approach to resource evaluation is a deliberately confected deception which has been consciously concocted to deceive, caution and skepticism are called for. So, while the present essay refers to conscious subterfuge which no doubt has succeeded on occasion, it needs to be appreciated that the spirituality-based sacralisation of landscape is a very real element of many Indigenous religions and should not be dismissed simply because it doesn't fit the western template for methodology or real data. With this caveat in mind, it is illuminating to give mature consideration to Widdowson's views in the Australian context.

While these contrarian authors were regarded as disrespectful racists by the protagonists of the cause of the Indigenes, their much-quoted use of the Emperor's New Clothes metaphor in this context, has given the cultural non-believers fresh wind in their sails. Whether the Emperor metaphor is an apt concept for assessment of cultural voracity, has been argued long and hard by the 'Get over it, get on with it' lobby on Aboriginal policy. Nevertheless, irrespective of how appropriate the Emperor's story is to contemporary Aboriginality, it offers a platform on which to examine cultural respect and tribal pride as a subset of the identity debate.

Lets refresh our minds on Hans Christian Anderson's 1837 original story 'The Emperor's New Clothes'. In essence this fable revolves around the way two con men deceived the Emperor, his minders and his people, into buying a suit of clothes which didn't actually exist. They do this using a two-stage strategy that first prohibits the questioning of the existence of the clothes, woven from a special silk and invisible to all but the weavers themselves. Having convinced the Emperor of this invisibility, which they maintain, only stupid people would query, they set up a weaver's workshop in the palace where they go through the motions of producing the cloth, pretending to pass the threads through the reciprocating loom until the imaginary clothes are complete. When the time for the fitting of the unseen garment arrives, a young child, unaware of the taboo of never questioning the invisibility of the clothes shouts, 'The Emperor has no clothes on!' The assembled attendants have no option but to believe their eyes – the Emperor is definitely naked.

The moral of this story which has been perpetuated for the best part of two centuries, is that human gullibility allows us to believe and promulgate concepts which are actually untrue. Widdowson and Howard maintain that it is our fear of ridicule and non-conformity which makes dissent from group-think difficult for most individuals.

Australians can judge from the frequent reference to the Emperor's New Clothes myth by media commentators, that the idea of being had for a sucker, is alive and well not only in the Aboriginal Industry but in other emerging issues such as our ability to affect climate change and terrorism. The Canadian mining example in 'Disrobing the Aboriginal Industry' is pertinent to our Australian Indigenous Rights situation and bears analysis here.

The Northwest Territories of Canada in the mid 1990's had to deal with a BHP application to mine diamonds in that frigid region. In 1993 the NWT government had constructed the world's first Traditional Knowledge Policy which mandated the inclusion of such knowledge, both experiential and spiritual, into government programs and services. In this way, Traditional Knowledge (TK) was accepted and respected by governments as a valid and essential source of information.

Few were surprised when the BHP consultants in anthropology, reported great difficulty in separating TK from its traditional cultural context. In the end, BHP surprised all participants of this unique situation, by agreeing to fund TK research without knowing what it actually was. In addition, BHP accepted Aboriginal demands that they, as First People, retain the propriety rights (intellectual property) over all TK studies' findings.

The plot thickened when the Department of Indian and Northern Affairs were shown to be incapable of demonstrating not only the methodology of TK, but importantly, how TK could be used in the Environmental Impact Assessment (EIA) of the proposed mine. There was, despite this anomaly, an assumption by the local Aborigines that a further increase in funds would be forthcoming to accumulate more special knowledge.

Attempts by BHP to combine TK with real scientific investigation of potential mining impacts, caused a high level of concern among the locals, that scientific knowledge systems could pose the real danger of destroying the cultural context of their TK. While it was clear to BHP Anthropologists that an ecological understanding of the physical process of mine operation and rehabilitation was essential, the locals made no attempt to accommodate this self-evident truism.

Widdowson and Howard were living in Northwest Territory at the time that the Panel mandated TK in the EIA. Up to that time, nobody regarded TK as a necessary element in the assessment process, let alone explaining just how TK would contribute. They asked questions publicly and privately at the review of the Panel's reporting sessions. It was the lack of logical answers to their incisive questioning which, in their words 'inadvertently uncovered the subterfuge'. What they regarded as 'extensive chicanery' was only the tip of an Emperor's clothes-type iceberg.

Despite the Department of Indian and Northern Affairs claiming that a 'huge database' of TK already existed and could be valuable in future research, on inspection of the records, no such database existed, except for boxes of tapes of unverified elders' anecdotes. In explanation of the queried value of this material, the defenders of TK stated that the cultural complexity of this information made it difficult to describe the significance of TK to outsiders. Nonetheless, Bill Erasmus, Grand Chief of the Aboriginal Dene nation, insisted that TK was in fact 'Dene Science'.

It is understandable that a senior tribal leader interprets the concept of 'science' in a way which is amenable to his TK. However, the regularity with which the TK/Science debate keeps emerging in land rights negotiations in several countries, makes it encumbent on the investigative scholar to revisit the basic assumptions of the TK defendants.

The first assumption seems to be the rather vaguely-defined personal status of the individual holding the TK, be he lawman, rainman, songman or medicineman. It is held that those who don't behave according to community norms cannot exercise this 'sacred' knowledge. In other words, only the good guys have TK. It is also firmly believed that TK is grounded in the native spirituality which forms the framework for the Indigenous worldview. Importantly, TK is based on the belief that the universe is governed by spiritual forces that cannot be seen by the white man.

This brings the analogy of invisible clothes sharply into focus and seems to add finality to the incompatibility of evidence-based science with the sharmanism of Aboriginality. It is this mystical and mythical purity of TK which seems to forever seal the incapacity of TK to make a verifiable contribution to policy formulation.

In the BHP case, the company was prevented by the rules of engagement from questioning the voracity of TK and associated beliefs – only ignorant people would query the actuality of the Emperor's new clothes.

Needless, to say, Australian Aborigines valued the progress of the Indigenous Rights struggle in Canada. However, the doubters of TK's positive role in evidence-based negotiations, began to worry about how the mysticism of TK's cultural context was starting to raise its head in Australian land rights negotiations. In time, this led to a more serious challenge to those elements of belief which were deemed 'beyond Whitefella comprehension'.

So once again, any hint of outsiders implying that spiritual subterfuge be exposed for what it is, was conveniently labelled as racist disrespect, lack of spiritual understanding and even cultural genocide – a handy term to stir the activists whose antennae were forever alert to right-wing fascists lurking in the shadows.

The real merits of the Australian Aboriginal cause have been dumbed down by the sophism (=false argument intended to deceive (Oxford)) of the cultural/mythical context of many claims, which could easily stand proud without the fabricated chicanery of the lawmen. The genuine land claims and proposals for self-governance don't need this sharmanic pillar to support them, nor do the informed leaders of Aboriginal thought on future options push this immature posturing.

So the publication of Widdowson and Howard's belief that they had exposed what they referred to as 'the ever-expanding parasitic Aboriginal Industry', predictably led to a range of opportunists either ducking for cover or taking the 'holier-than-thou' stance of the morally offended. What has happened in the past decade of land claims in Australia, has been largely confected by lawyers, consultants, academics, clergy and moral do-gooders in the media. The voice of the people has been drowned out by the righteous busybodies who make it their self-appointed business to beat the identity drum and cry foul whenever humanitarian reason raises its head.

There needs to be a distinction made between what the Aboriginal Industry have constructed as a refuge from reality and what Aborigines really need. There is little argument that it is education, skills and productive values which will enable young Aborigines to survive and prosper in the modern world. However, those who continue to insist that the only true path to self-esteem through traditional identity, is by exaggerating the need for a return to country with its customary ceremonies and norms, would do well to re-assess their worldview.

Somewhere between the mystical sharmanism of the past, and the insensitive disrespect for cultural appreciation, is a broad-minded tolerance of a functioning multiculture. The 'live and let live' acceptance of cultural difference is a universally-held aspiration which can do without the outdated absolutism of the Dark Ages, be it Aboriginal or European. Any further pretence that the Age of Reason is not yet upon us, should be met with the scorn it deserves, and its advocates should be prevented from damaging yet another generation of First People. In doing this, those powerful families who have been siphoning off their people's funds for generations, should be held to account.

Widdowson's investigations have uncovered what he calls 'a greater and more harmful deception' than the BHP case referred to. In his words: 'It obscures the unprecedented and special character of the circumstances facing Aboriginal People.' He reminds us that the gap in cultural advancement at the time of first contact, came when Europeans were transitioning from feudalism to capitalism. At that time the most primitive 'chipping and flaking technologies' of the Neolithic Age, were also moving to a 'grinding and polishing' phase, setting the scene for transition from Stone to Bronze to Iron Age. In simple terms, anthropologists recognised parallel social changes through three phases from Savagery to Barbarism to Civilisation, the latter being characterised by literacy.

Jarod Diamond has written extensively on this matter of how we interpret 'the gap' between cultures. The misconception that Aborigines today are still at their earlier neolithic (rock-based) stage of development, is a widely-held mindset which remains alive and well in right-wing circles. The point has often been made that many Indigenous People in a range of climates, have drifted toward being consumers rather than producers. Reference to the perpetuation of neolithic social mores usually brings cries of 'racist bigot', but it is hard to explain undisciplined work habits, tribal identification, animistic beliefs and defective development of abstract cognition, in any other way. The fact that these features have endured through centuries of exposure to modernity, says something about how deeply certain inherited human traits are embedded in the brain.

It is the gap in capacity for cultural adaptation, rather than the oft-quoted loss of culture, which will eventually explain lagging standards of well-being in many of the world's Indigenous Peoples. Those whose habit of perpetuating colonial trauma to their offspring, would do their mob a favour if they'd take this funda-mental distinction between the 'adoptive gap' and their favoured conviction of cultural genocide to heart, and act accordingly. There are many Aboriginal communities who experienced only minimal disruption to their culture, who still exhibit a damaging incapac-ity to take up modern opportunities. These groups, mainly in the Top End and Cape York, need help with adaptive well-being, not cultural resurrection, as promulgated by the shallow martyrists whose only tool is the 'Poor Fella Me' syndrome.

Aboriginal leaders must now speed-up their choice between Widdowson's 'critical eye or bleeding heart' if the causes and corrective actions for their people's plight are to form the basis for their progress.

DOES FAIR GO
NEED REDEFINITION?

In a remarkable piece in The Monthly (August 2015) Noel Pearson reckons the constitutional recognition shambles is all the fault of government putting too much emphasis on process rather than on principle or policy. He describes the current confusion as follows: 'The political and policy cacophony in social and traditional media is too much for the mob to absorb and understand. There is simply too much happening.' The public, says one pollster, need to be able to cling onto process – they need a mirage of order in an increasingly uncertain world.

Pearson doesn't take any personal blame for the contemporary confusion and he doesn't admit to the number of times he has made additional submissions to the constitutional change clearing-house. As a member of the original Expert Panel he made a detailed early submission on change proposals back in 2011. This was a comprehensive and well-researched document which also proposed two new Acts on Aboriginal language and a new consultative body. He was apparently unable to convince his Panel colleagues to adopt his ideas, so he set about producing at least two more submissions.

Pearson's next contribution was to the Kirribilli House meeting of 40 Indigenous leaders with the Prime Minister and Opposition Leader, when he made two proposals. The first was to enshrine constitutional recognition in legislation before an election. He reminded the Prime Minister that Section 128 of the Constitution states that referendums must be held between two and six months after the change in legislation has been passed. Such legislation would finalise the referendum question(s) and would trigger the holding of the referendum. His second proposal was the holding of an Indigenous plebiscite on the referendum question(s), aimed at reaching an Indigenous consensus.

During the Kirribilli meeting, Abbott and Shorten came up with two proposals of their own, which had not been part of the day's discussion: One was that community conferences be held (no reference to Indigenous conferences); the other was also a 'new' idea, i.e. that a Referendum Council had in fact already been recommended in late 2014 by a Government Review Panel. In addition, Pearson then challenged the Parliamentary Joint Select Committee under MP Ken Wyatt, to explain why they agreed to make recommendations which they knew 'had no chance of bipartisan support'. The suspicion that the Non-discriminatory clause in the Constitution would be interpreted as a Bill of Rights, would scare the horses in the mainstream and would sink this proposal politically.

At the same time as Pearson was complaining about the process, Gary Johns and Murray Walters were complaining about Pearson. Johns, in a none-too-subtle attack on Pearson under the heading 'Pearson's Peerage: A Proposal to Entrench the Incentive to Complain' (Quadrant July 2015) omits any praise of Pearson's successes and goes straight for Pearson's proposal for an Indigenous Representative Body which, according to Johns, was first dubbed a House of Lords by Aboriginal leaders. Naming a new group in the Constitution would hand Australia a privileged Band with an incentive to complain and no way of abolition [of that body], says

Johns. He's a little harsh when he claims that Aborigines have been granted special privileges such as land grants and funded programs on the basis of race, more fashionably termed indigeneity or first people or culture. All fair-minded Australians with a sense of honest history would know that 'privilege' is hardly the correct connotation for these policies.

Johns' second beef is Pearson's repeated claim that 'we have no voice' in policy-making. Johns maintains that, for a minority, Aborigines have many voices, and endless opportunities to put their case to government. Perhaps Pearson's problem is not 'no voice' but 'no listening'. But even that may be inaccurate, when what he really means is that what is listened to, is rarely taken seriously, let alone adopted. Johns then returns to his pertinent question, 'Who is an Aborigine?'. He asks how distinctive this (70% out-marrying) group needs to be, to warrant a special and extra voice. His inference is that this non-distinctive group's call for a special voice rings hollow. This view accords with this author's original paper on policy in 1998 titled 'What Constitutes a Fair Go for Aborigines?'. Murray Walters, a Brisbane psychiatrist (*Quadrant Online* 08/07/2015) picks up on some of the above points under the editor's stirring title of 'Poignancy, Pathos and Constitutional Piffle'. He's referring to Pearson's claim in the press that Aborigines 'need a lot more than symbolism'.

Walters refers to Pearson's recent writings about how he watched his family's children playing on the beach in Cape York and hunting in the nearby mangroves, inferring this is how it was and how it should be for future generations. Walters maintains that Pearson has less chance and no more right, to see his vision fulfilled than do the rest of us. 'The nation doesn't owe Pearson his dreaming' Murray claims, minimising the impact and trauma of dispossession.

Commenting on Pearson's reference to his people crossing the Torres Strait landbridge 53K years ago, Walters suggests that Pearson's actual connection to these ancients 'manifests a popular collective fantasy' and says this pathos shouldn't be used as support for constitutional change. He joins Johns when he says 'And please, no more of this 'voices' thing'. Walters asks whether it is racist to expect more of leaders such as Mick Dodson who seem prone to criticise non-Aboriginal leaders as racist. 'There seems to be a real problem with several Aboriginal leaders confusing symbolic thinking with reality. The last thing we need is more of other peoples idealism written across our [mainstream] lives,' says Walters.

The revered 'fair go' idea probably requires re-consideration as a contemporary Australianism. The reason for a re-think was illustrated by Johns (The Australian 30/12/2014) when advocating his controversial 'no contraception, no benefits' proposal: A single mother in Cairns with nine children from five fathers, was drawing child support for each of her brood. When queried about the morality of this in the press, an Aboriginal activist Gracelyn Smallwood, called for a 24 hour taxpayer-funded culturally-appropriate service for such mothers. Johns' conclusion is that these people are 'breeding strife'. Fair Go?

All the above criticisms may be assuming that Pearson speaks for most Aborigines and has wide support. The truth is that for two decades he's been careful to clarify that he spoke only for his Cape York people, specifically, for the 13 clans on the East coast. It was only in 2015 that he spread his constituency to a national level in his Empowering Communities report. As yet we haven't seen the government's response to that report, which is a pity because Pearson regards it as his seminal contribution to Aboriginal well-being.

This brings us to the basic question of how to match government (mainstream?) and Aboriginal aspirations. There is something of a split in the Aboriginal ranks on the question of separate development and whether integration is all bad. There is also division on whether, to maintain self-esteem, it is necessary to allow one's Aboriginal identity to define one's values and lifestyle. In addition, the matter of whether discrimination is actually based almost solely on colour, appears to be unresolved. So when one of our popular Aboriginal singers calls for 'more people of colour' on television and stage, the mainstream probably have no problem with that. Jimmy Little and Seaman Dan never had racial problems and were accepted for their innate talent. So why did an AFL player recently receive the thumbs down when he demanded respect for his origin?

Much as we would like to think that the mainstream are neutral on colour, there is ample evidence that many employers are not colour-neutral. This means that when Aborigines are encouraged to 'learn and earn', they may still have reason to expect a degree of discrimination in many sectors of society. If the mainstream don't understand why 'authentic' Aborigines prefer separate development, they need look no further than this. It is for this reason that the call to integrate doesn't always ring true and won't be credible until acceptance and general equity become a reality.

The challenge for both government and Aborigines, is to find ways of enlivening Pearson's Empowerment program in a way which provides an economic base, without the negative affects of 'allowing us to be ourselves'. At least not to the extent that it reduces up-and-coming generations' capacity to join modern Australia. This means caution in accepting as necessarily positive, the call to 'stop trying to change us into people we are not'. Adaptation and integration are not an all-or-nothing change in values, rather they are a gradual and nuanced series of positive modifications of lifestyle and behavioural norms. Let's build on the best of Aboriginal heritage and avoid the worst of modern habits.

As Pearson emphasises in his report, personal empowerment rather than group empowerment, is an essential facet of progress, which is why Empowered Individuals appear in his title. It is for this reason that Aborigines would do well to re-think the role of collectivism in planning their society's future. Most people would be aware that there is probably more variation in behavioural norms within the Aboriginal communities (80% of whom are urbanised) than between them and other ethnic groups. This also accounts for the way in which thousands of light-skinned families have played down their Aboriginal heritage and joined the non-Aboriginal majority. It may also be the reason why so many Aboriginal leaders have chosen to marry non-Aboriginal spouses.

In practice, Australia appears to operate on an accepted but unspoken dichotomy of Black Pride and White Dominance, both of which have reasons for their self-esteem. Between these two positions is that great Australian migrant mob, which Nino Culotta described so well in his 1960's book 'They're a Weird Mob'. Admittedly he was reflecting the European migrant's view of the Australians, although his theme of 'live and let live' is a masterpiece of pub-talk and includes how to take a 'sickie' and get yourself declared disabled.

And what's this all got to do with a Fair Go? The message is that much can be achieved for Aboriginal well-being without changing the Constitution. All it needs is *earned* mutual respect.

RECOGNISE MORE THAN FIRST PEOPLE

One thing Australian politics is good at is thinking up slogans to encapsulate a complex idea in one, two or three words. Often the possible interpretations are so ambiguous that every group, irrespective of their ideology, feel that the slogan speaks to them and supports their cause. In the process, individuals warm to the slogans because they're motherhood stuff, they're Australian, they're fair dinkum and they meet the central criterion of a fair go – what mates do.

The latest one-word slogan is 'RECOGNISE', originally meant to convey national agreement that the Aborigines were this country's First People and, as such, should be acknowledged in the nation's founding document. Anyone who has read the pamphlets, posters and stickers put out by the Liberally-funded RECOGNISE office, will be aware that the aim is to go beyond simply recognising First People constitutionally, and to include respect for their Indigenous culture, language, stories, ways of valuing ancestor country, respecting myths and Genesis beliefs.

With the predictable argy-bargy which has arisen during the search for constitutional wording, it has become clear that fuzzy thinking on objectives of the whole RECOGNISE procedure, has led to an unholy row between clans, language groups and self-appointed spokespersons.

At the risk of being branded an ignorant outsider with no

understanding of Indigenous values, culture or tradition, I suggest that a new list of the things we should RECOGNISE, be put to the group responsible for drawing up the wording for a national referendum.

Australians should be asked to tick the 'yes' or 'no' box on recognition of the following concepts in an effort to gain consensus on the place and role of Aborigines in the future Australian nation:

1. **RECOGNISE** that we were all cavemen once and that we're all migrants.

2. **RECOGNISE** that Aborigines were the first humans to inhabit this continent.

3. **RECOGNISE** that after 50,000 years of occupation, the Aborigines were still hunter-gatherer cavemen at the time of first contact.

4. **RECOGNISE** that global migrations historically led to newcomers dominating original inhabitants.

5. **RECOGNISE** that fairness or legality were never criteria by which successful migrations by newcomers were judged.

6. **RECOGNISE** that advances in technical and intellectual capacity were always what characterised migrating newcomers who intervened in the original inhabitant's way of life.

7. **RECOGNISE** that invaded peoples only became subservient to newcomers when they lacked the military power to resist and overcome the newcomers.

8. **RECOGNISE** that world history demonstrates that invasion is driven by a desire to gain new resources of many different types.

9. **RECOGNISE** that the march of human civilisations is based on adopting new ideas, new values and new technology, a process accelerated by infusion of new cultures.

10. **RECOGNISE** that culture is not civilisation, that physical structures and civil organisations have arisen from a dissatisfaction with the primitive *status quo* and recognition of the advantages of civil advancement in benefiting both individuals and groups.

11. **RECOGNISE** that personal productivity in its many forms, is the key to group progress and that without wealth-generation, group well-being stagnates.

12. **RECOGNISE** that respect from others cannot be legally enforced or demanded, but must be earned by behaviour and performance which meet community norms.

13. **RECOGNISE** that racial separatism cannot deliver the same level of advancement as diverse unity can, built on tolerant co-operation.

14. **RECOGNISE** that each group of migrants can maintain their identity and enjoy their culture, without losing their common national aspirations as one of the world's most successful multicultures.

15. **RECOGNISE** that personal progress depends on our capacity to adapt, to change, to value new ways and to appreciate that not all our traditional beliefs are useful, appropriate or beneficial in our children's modern world.

16. **RECOGNISE** that, while respect and comfort for our elders are honourable sentiments which should be preserved, it is the future of our coming generations which determines our success as a group.

17. **RECOGNISE** that while teaching our youth the traditional knowledge of their country can be an appropriate segment of our education policy, a mature balance between idealism and reality is required if coming generations are to develop into competitive moderns.

18. **RECOGNISE** that while mother-tongue language has deep emotive roots which strengthen our sense of belonging, the appropriate role and function of global language can be ignored only at our peril.

19. **RECOGNISE** that most health problems result from personal choices and that even expensive healthcare fails when individual responsibility fails.

20. **RECOGNISE** that the current definition of Aboriginality is fraught and insufficient to act as a binding thread for identity and organisational purposes.

21. **RECOGNISE** that highly variable dominance of Aboriginal DNA cannot continue to be used as an 'opt-in' criterion for group membership, and because of this policy weakness, it must be replaced by the concept of 'need' rather than genetic association, as the basis for supportive welfare policy.

22. **RECOGNISE** that for historic reasons, there is a degree of tension between the world's races and religions, and that expecting a non-discriminatory worldwide brotherhood, is at odds with human tendencies which cause common language and faith to draw individuals together.

23. **RECOGNISE** that we don't need to love our neighbours but we do need to tolerate them, as they tolerate us.

24. **RECOGNISE** that each human group has a collective responsibility to the earth on which we depend, and for

this reason population growth, pollution control and resource maintenance are everyone's responsibility and should be taught in homes and schools.

25. **RECOGNISE** that group identity in most young nations is not a clear-cut phenomenon, and as such, all citizens should learn to tolerate uncertainty, respect change and practice patience.

PART THREE

Religion and Spirituality

VALUING INDIGENOUS SPIRITUALITY

I am one of the many Australian writers who are guilty of serious generalization when attempting to describe and appreciate Aboriginal religion. While there are certain core features, such as the Rainbow Serpent, which seem to run throughout the many tribal variations of the Dreamtime stories, it is the local variations and additions which are of central importance in distinguishing tribes and even clans, and in providing a distinctive identity to the members concerned. Together with language or 'lingo', the unique stories, songlines and ceremonies of the group are what give tribal adherents their sense of belonging, of family and of their own ancestral country.

A cursory study of the world's remaining indigenous peoples, shows several common features which characterize them as Indigenous or First People:

i.   They're close to the Earth and revere Mother Nature as their nurturer.
ii. They value and maintain close family ties which involve family loyalty, duty and responsibility.
iii. They are largely self-sufficient and thus independent, provided they have access to sufficient natural resources.
iv. They are spiritual by nature, maintaining great respect for both their ancestors and the Earth Spirits.

v. They derive inner strength, persistence and on-going resilience from their unshakeable beliefs, customs and traditions.

The indigenes of the Australian continent are blessed with an additional element of their genesis and that is the unparalleled antiquity of their people. Before 'Mungo Man', Aborigines were thought to have been in the Great Southland for a few thousand years. Jim Bowdler's findings at Lake Mungo pushed this estimate out beyond 20 000 years and since then reliable evidence of 50 000 year-old sites has been recorded

At first contact in the late 1700s, the newcomers had no understanding, let alone appreciation of the significance of what they referred to as the primitive Animism of the locals. Later when the Christian missions were set up, there was a concerted effort to convert the Aborigines to 'the one true religion'. The methods used varied from benign persuasion, through what could only be called 'spiritual bribery' using food and other favours, to downright cruelty and harsh punishment for non-cooperators. Over time, the original assumption that these stone-age people would die out as the Neanderthals had, gave way to acceptance of the resilience of the Aborigines. This resilience appeared to be based on the inner strength which these land-based people apparently drew from their clan country and its spiritual/ancestral bonds. By the 1980's this seemingly unbreakable bond to country caused the government to recognize the need for Native Title over many areas of tribal land where artifacts and paintings proved the antiquity of owner-ship. Over time, many mainstream Australians very slowly started becoming aware of the deep significance of the stories, songlines and ceremonies of the dispossessed.

This essay attempts to examine the origin and meaning of 'Aboriginal religion' – a term only vaguely comprehended by outsiders, but a field of study which has had the attention of Anthropologists, Theologists, Sociologists and others in the human sciences since the late 19th century.

Aboriginal Beliefs

The first aspect of Indigenous Spirituality which strikes the serious scholar, is the wide geographical variation in the Dreamtime stories among the hundreds of language groups occupying clearly defined tribal countries. The absence of holy scriptures complicates comparisons with other religions whose Bible, Koran or Tora, offer a basis for interpretation. Not that Australian Aborigines are the only global Indigenous people to rely on the oral tradition of knowledge transfer.

The writer does not intend to compare the various contributors' interpretations of Aboriginal religiosity, but rather attempts to unpack the common threads of belief. Perhaps one of the best previous attempts to do this, was that of Ronald Berndt, who produced a masterly piece of research for the Australian Society for Theological studies in 1979. The earlier work of A.P. Elkin, W.E.H. Stanner and A.R. Radcliffe-Brown all contributed to our understanding of Aboriginal mythology, philosophy, morality, ethics, rites, obligations and totemism. So too, did those converted Aboriginal clerics whose personal understanding of the interface between Christianity and Animism, helped us to identify the 'useful' elements of comparative religions. No attempt is made here to repeat the author's earlier analysis of the merits of the Christian Missions, published under the title 'Missionaries: Heroes or Villains'.

Berndt points out that as scholars we tend instinctively to evaluate other religions within the framework of our own religious upbringing and in doing this, there may be an unconscious assumption about the truth and thus value, of our home brand.

Many writers, but especially Carl Strehlow, the father of the Hermannsberg religious philosophy, have remarked on the powerful ancestral and spiritual obligations which our tribal people responded to in their way of life and their reverence for the landscape. However, few analysts have attempted to explain and appreciate the extent to which this sacred view of land, water, plants and animals, has provided an unshakable life force and a personal dedication to all that is sacrosanct.

There appear to be three relationships which constitute Aboriginal core beliefs:

i.   Relations between humans themselves.
ii. Between humans and nature.
iii. Between humans and deities.

It is this three-way linkage which forms the basis for what in English has become known as the 'Dreaming'.

I suspect that the words 'Dreaming' and 'Dreamtime' are insufficient and probably inaccurate in the image they convey about an ancient, spiritual, ancestral process by which Man's identity and sense of belonging is eternally established.

What the Aboriginal religion has done, is not only 'humanised' the world in which they live, but has offered a lasting foundation for their social order. The mythical characters which are recognised as the creators of the landscape, form the basis of belief in the sacred and in the sacred power invested in them. The belief that Man and

Nature are one, is no different from the ancient Tao belief – a concept taken on by modern conservationists or Deep Ecologists. The persistent mandala which calls for a return to Nature, has its roots in Indigenous philosophy. The Man/Land harmony which chief Seattle is credited with elucidating, finds support all over the modern world. Since the 1930's the credo of Aldo Leopold in the US, has been the recognition of the Community of Man and Nature.

In their pre-colonial state, the Aborigines may be regarded as sacred people, a people whose religious beliefs constantly guided their every-day lives. From these beliefs sprang rituals and from rituals, their behaviours and social mores developed. Social rules in turn, determined how members of the family 'moiety' related to each other.

By spiritualising their natural world, the Aborigines are given a sense of permanence, of symbiosis, of belonging and obligation; all of which contribute to a resilient individual identity and a unified community bound by common beliefs.

Unsurprisingly, the beliefs and stories of people in very different habitats, vary markedly. So, it should be expected that the stories of the physically different dwellers of the Western Desert with their harsh drought survival tactics, have little in common with the permanently well-nourished tribes of the fruitful coastal estuaries. While the disdain shown by pampered European critics for the treatment of infants and the elderly in desert communities is predictable, the almost unparalleled survival capacities of these people cannot be denied.

In his masterful evaluation of Aboriginal religion, Berndt makes no mention of the extent to which their beliefs have affected Aborigines' willingness and ability to come out of their stone-age thought-patterns and to adapt to modernity. Such an effect of Indigenous religion may seem beyond the ambit of this essay, but in contemporary Australia the material influence of different religions may have a somewhat greater effect on individual well-being than first thought. This aspect of Aboriginal spirituality may focus on whether or not the belief in predetermined 'destiny' guides personal behaviour. Such a belief may well demotivate individuals from improving their situation. In the same way the evangelists preached to Christian converts: 'Everything is in God's hands; He determines our fate.' While such spiritual shifting of personal responsibility can be comforting, too much acceptance of preordained destiny, does nothing for advancement of well-being. Similarly, unless discontent with the *status quo* moves individuals to seek a better life for their families, stagnation is virtually guaranteed. Unless bread-winners actually believe in 'free choice' as a means of betterment, the gap between the 'haves' and the 'have nots' is likely to widen.

What was the Missionary Effect?

It has to be admitted that most, perhaps almost all, of the various Christian Missions were both ignorant and dismissive of the spiritual virtues of Aboriginal religion. [See next essay for an exception.] Berndt's wide-ranging evidence strongly suggests that both missionaries and Aborigines were blinded by their own religion. For both groups, changing the basic tenets of their respective religions seemed quite out of the question. The opportunity to find spiritual commonality was never seized, probably never even seriously considered.

What were the reasons why the Christian theologians hardly ever acknowledged the positive elements of Aboriginal spirituality?

Firstly, they must have had an unmovable conviction of the truth of their own religious myths. Secondly, they had a conversion job to do; so their success was measured in the number of baptisms. Thirdly, they were imbued with a moral superiority which never considered that primitive pagans could have any deserved place in comparative religions.

The outcomes of the Australian Mission effort were patchy at best. Apart from teaching what the clergy regarded as 'civilizing influences' such as clothes, hygiene, food production, literacy and religious instruction, the simultaneous planned destruction of native religiosity and its attendant identity generally led to secularisation rather than conversion. Not to gainsay the number of Aborigines who did become practicing church-going Christians, the great majority of Mission inmates were left in limbo, with no spiritual roots or grounding.

Today's secular humanitarians might welcome such a deity-free situation as being in line with modern values. They might welcome the removal of what they regard as the 'shackles of religion' of whatever colour. However, if we look deeper into the heartfelt attempts of a minority of missionaries, we do find isolated efforts to identify what they considered to be the most valuable (useful) aspects of Indigenous spirituality. It appears that certain clerics saw a parallel between the Creative Beings of the Dreamtime and the Old Testament Prophets, both of whom pre-dated Christ and the Gospels. In practice, there are churches today all over the Top End, Cape York and Torres Strait which proudly display the tokens and icons of both religions. Theirs is a vibrant and vigorous hybrid community whose church services would disappoint both the High Church and the Dreamtime Purists.

These 'home-made' churches have not gone as far as Dawkins

(of 'The God Delusion' fame) who invented his own Command-ments for humanitarians, but they have done a bit of picking and choosing from the tenets of Aboriginal beliefs and have moulded a useful supportive home-grown set of principles for their flocks.

Even in the early days of missionary endeavour, some such as the Methodist Awareness Mission worked on the principle of 'keeping what is best' (Berndt) in the local culture all along the coast of Arnhem Land where they'd established a string of stations. Their attempts to maintain the Mission Aborigines' contact with their clan country, also bore fruit and was starkly contrasted against most of the other 'unbending' missions who could see nothing but evil in the locals' ceremonies.

Contemporary Spirituality

Today there are increasing signs of a split in the Aboriginal ranks, between what I'd call the traditionalists and the modernists. This split is not fundamentally a religious divide, but rather a broader lifestyle/well-being choice. Some would claim that the modernists are abandoning their ancestral obligations and personal responsibility to country. The other side would claim that unthinking devotion to tradition in the homelands, is selling the next generations short in terms of opportunities to benefit from mainstream well-being.

Contemporary Australia has to deal with an 80% urbanised Aboriginal population plus a remote minority whose geographical spread and isolation largely preclude cost-effective health and education services. In common with the Amerindians of Canada and the US, Indigenous Australians are seeking a future which encompasses the best of both worlds. Unsurprisingly, Indigenous leaders who tend to overplay or underplay the significance of custom and tradition, are caught between a rock and a hard place when challenged in the public square.

The complexity of the interaction between religion, land rights, income generation and identity, means that developing an agreed majority view on optional futures is extremely difficult. My research, across twenty years, suggests that aspiring to a single homogenous Indigenous identity and sense of values, is not only unrealistic, but will delay the inevitable acceptance of a flexible, heterogeneous solution which encompasses a nuanced Indigenous identity reflecting individual free choice.

Such a grab-bag of loyalties, of belongings, of responsibilities and of answers to 'who am I?' can be schizophrenic or enabling, even empowering, depending on the individual's strength of character and independence, or the need for an emotional crutch.

The harsh cold legal processes of Native Title determinations apply Whitefella Law to Blackfella country, but they do respect the continuity of clan occupation of ancestral lands, ancient links to country and spiritual connectivity. When PM Whitlam poured sand into the hand of Vincent Lingiari at the Wave Hill Handover, for the very first time the White leadership demonstrated its understanding of the real meaning of sacred ground to this ancient land-centred culture. Long may this belated appreciation continue to grow.

ABORIGINAL DEBT
TO THE STREHLOWS

I have elsewhere asked the question: Were the missionaries heroes or villains? Because the record of achievements of the Australian mission-field is so variable and the criteria for gauging success are so political, glaring examples abound at both ends of the spectrum. Among the ruins of the Christian evangelical effort, one family shines as a beacon above the rest, at least on the issue of understanding Aboriginal culture.

Three generations of the Strehlow family at Hermannsberg, west of Alice Springs, have left this nation with a unique insight into the real meaning of Aboriginal songlines, ceremonies and inflections of language. From this emerged a fresh appreciation of cultural values which eluded the mainstream anthropologists, Anglo missionaries and official protectors.

The story starts with Carl Strehlow and his devotion to the people of the Western Desert over a period of thirty years (1894-1922). Carl published his eight volume work 'The Aranda and Loritja Tribes of Central Australia' in 1908, written in German, printed in Frankfurt and never translated into English.

This work probably formed the personal philosophical basis for Carl's anthropologist son Ted, who laboured until 1971 before he published his massive (800 page) 'Songs of Central Australia'. In reviewing Ted's work, it is described by Nicholas Rothwell (Australian 11/2/14) as 'the only book to bring a Classical sensibility to Aboriginal song poetry. Finally John Strehlow, grandson of Carl, completes the family narrative with his amazing 'The Tale of Frieda Keysser', Carl's wife whose superhuman efforts to diarise daily life at Hermannsberg, left a detailed account of the Strehlow interaction with the Aranda and others. The story of how Frieda fled with her diaries from the Red Army when they entered Berlin, and how she had earlier protected the diaries against the 1910 floods in Oodnadatta, gives Frieda's story a special significance. With renowned German thoroughness, John persisted for 17 years to produce his 1200 page Tale. Rothwell, admires it as a 'painstaking reconstruction of the past and an intense questioning of today's conventional wisdom…'.

The importance of the Strehlow's unique family story, lies not only in its portrayal of the era when contrasting philosophies on Aboriginal futures brought Carl, then Ted, into serious conflict with pastoralists, but also in its enlightened appreciation of a culture dismissed as primitive by others. Some historians wonder whether the Aranda would have survived if it were not for the strong and persistent support and advocacy of the Hermannsberg Lutherans. If ever a monument of acknowledgement by Aborigines was deserved, this is it.

With the place of the Strehlows in Aboriginal culture firmly established, Anna Kenny in 2013 produced 'The Aranda's Pepa' which further ensconces their position in Australian anthropology. While readership of Kenny's rather specialised genre is probably limited, its popular assessment by the Adelaide reviewer Gary Clark (Quadrant June, 2015) reveals the real significance of their historic effort.

Under the title of 'What Australia Owes the Strehlows', Clark unveils the true understanding which Carl exhibited in 'Tribes' and then so effectively built on by Ted in his 'Songs'. Clark goes on to remind us that 'Songs' is not only a genuine masterpiece of Australian prose, but is writing which has had more impact on our literary culture than on our anthropology. Kenny believes that Carl was unique in the way he employed the earlier German Romantic tradition when valuing Aboriginal language and culture. Clark reminds us that it was Gertrude Levy, in her well-known cave-art interpretation titled 'The Gate of Horn' in 1947, who pointed out that Aboriginal spirituality resembled that of the Greeks and Romans. These civilisations also revered the underworld of dreams and ancestors, and the emergence of spirit-beings from caves or from underground.

This was the first time that 'primitive' Aboriginal beliefs had been associated with Classics such as Virgil's 'Aeneid' in which Aeneas descends into the underworld, via the cave of Cumae. Kenny tells us that in his 'Interpretation of Dreams', even Freud highlighted this underworld episode. The Aranda believe that many landscape features and sacred sites are traces of ancestors' journeys. When Ted wrote his 'Aranda Traditions' in 1943, he reflected an understanding of how and why the Aborigines are so closely bound to their clan country, an insight never before appreciated by Western anthropology.

Ted explains how the Aranda word meaning 'full of longing to return home', had previously been misinterpreted or even dismissed by Anglo specialists such as Baldwin Spencer and Francis Gillen, two of Australia's leading early anthropologists. These two had produced 'The Native Tribes of Central Australia' in 1899 but they missed, not only the irrepressible drive of the Aranda to return to home country, but also missed what Clark calls the 'aesthetic qualities [of Aranda song and ceremony] rivaling those of the Nordic sagas or Shakespeare'.

Because the Aranda language was a mother tongue to Ted as a child, his insight into the nuances and emotions of the language, gave him a depth of insight and empathy which were beyond the reach of Spencer and Gillen, who gained only a shallow and twisted interpretation from elders whose grasp of English was past tenuous. These institutionalised scientists were not amenable to the poetic way in which the Aranda's identify with their clan country as explained by Ted: 'The whole countryside is his living, age-old family tree. The story of his own totemic ancestor, is to the native, the account of his own doings at the beginning of time, at the dim dawn of life, when the world as he knows it now, was being shaped and moulded by all-powerful hands. He clings to his native soil with every fibre of his being. He will always speak of his own birthplace with love and reverence.' So Ted wasn't surprised that the Aranda had a special word meaning 'filled with longing to return home'.

Clark is of the opinion that the real value of Ted's work is that, unlike any other observer, he humanises the Aranda's art and he is uniquely able to demonstrate how their art 'expresses the riches of Aranda emotional life.

Ted's greatest challenge was the rise of Social Darwinism as exemplified by James Frazer's 'The Golden Bough' which developed the notion that technological progress (such as from wooden spears to iron steam-engines) ran parallel with mental evolution. In this way the anthropologists of the day regarded Aranda culture as clear evidence of an earlier stage of human development or evolution. This assumption precluded the belief that these 'primitives' could include aesthetics of any contemporary value. It must be said, as Clark did, that the Strehlows' approach to Aranda culture 'signalled a shift from the study of Aboriginal people as *objects* of *scientific* interest to subjects of their own unique kind of religious and aesthetic experience' (my italics).

In a strange twist of history, we have the Strehlows convinced that the Aranda could survive and adapt to the changes brought by first contact, while the other anthropologists accused them of contaminating the pure noble savage by preaching Christian beliefs which the Darwinists regarded as unscientific. In this contest of ideas, personal prejudice and professional jealousy were easy to deduce, as the Strehlows had a very intimate understanding of the native culture, which Spencer, Gillen and Fraser did not have. Professionally, Clark surmises that the Spencer camp reacted so negatively to the Strehlows because of Spencer's well-publicised theories on evolution. Carl had also recorded his personal doubts about Spencer's shallow and erroneous view of 'primitive' culture. Meanwhile in Europe at that time, Carl had gained wide support, even to the extent that the influential Marcel Mauss was of the opinion that Carl's published work was akin to what he termed 'an Aranda Rig Veda, equivalent to the ancient Hindu chants. Clark remarks that this assigned significance could equally be applied to Ted's even greater contribution.

Kenny emphasises, as no reviewer has done before, that the reputation of Carl's 'Tribes' as a significant contributor to Australian literature and archaeology, was recognised thanks largely to Carl's correspondence with Baron von Leonhardi, a researcher based in Germany. Unlike Carl who was working in the isolation of Hermannsburg, the Baron had studied all the contemporary anthropologists' work and could relate Carl's 'Tribes' to comparable studies. It was within this framework that the Baron acted as editor of Carl's final manuscript, so that when it was published in 1908, it contained an up-to-date catalogue of the strengths and weaknesses of competing theories on evolution of culture and man/land relationships. Before publication, the Baron had suggested that Carl re-interrogate the Aranda elders on a number of issues to confirm and strengthen the case which Carl's writings were making against the assumptions of the Darwinites in their assessment of Aboriginal culture and language.

The final draft of Carl's work represented the single most deeply informed treatise of that era on Aboriginal religion and natural intellect. It has also been heralded as the most detailed evaluation of native language ever undertaken in Australia. According to Kenny, the year before Carl died, he repudiated the claim that the Aranda's simple technology reflected a limited intellectual life. 'Never!' said Carl. Social Darwinism in the late 1800's ranked human cultures on a progressive ladder of achievement, each step coinciding with advances in civilisation. The German adoptees of Romanticism saw things differently, and they opposed the overt rationalism of Europe's own Enlightenment. They followed the teachings of Johan von Herder (1744-1803) who was reputed to have influenced Goethe before he became famous. Von Herder and the ensuing Romanticism movement which swept Europe, constituted a firm intellectual base for Carl's work.

Kenny's interpretation of the Baron's contribution to framing Carl's work in strong relativity, includes the deep emotional analysis of self, in a way that used the ancient folk culture and its poetry, to define living cultures. So beside drawing on Virgil, Goethe and the Brothers Grimm, the Romantics built a convincing alternative to the rational enlightenment and the emerging science of evolution. They were not denying physical evolution of brain and body, rather they found additional values in language, myth and their own powerful folklore.

Those opposing Carl's newfound sense of Aboriginal values, discounted his excellence as a student of Latin and Greek when he'd studied at the Neuendettelsau seminary. There, theology and culture acknowledged the history and values of potential converts in the missionfield. With this background, his appreciation of cultures very different from his own, was markedly at odds with that of the Anglo-Australian Darwinians. Where they saw evolutionary backwardness, Carl saw a richness, a strongly-held land-based faith and an unparalleled spirituality. He appreciated the deeper meaning of myths, especially when they were related in an ancient ecological language beyond the ken of mere rationalists. His insight was not an uninformed dismissal of the primitive, but a comparison and a rich probing of the Classics in which Greek and Roman mythology offer individuals and peoples a well-understood grounding, far removed from the physical evidence required by science. Importantly he was able to develop in his thinking, a clear connection between what Kenny calls 'dream-life and religious experience'. In addition, despite his ingrained Lutheranism, he didn't regard the Jesus story as the only authentic story. This theological open-mindedness apparently didn't diminish his personal Reformist faith, but rather reflected a level of Christian charity, of doing unto others, which was absent from the arrogance of the nominal Christianity of the Darwinians. The latters' view was that evolutionarily inferior races would become extinct for lack of competitive capacity. So it is not surprising that in his day, Carl was ostracised by the Anglo mainstream scientists.

Kenny is adamant about the uniqueness of Carl's stand: 'Save for the work of Roheim, also at Hermannsburg shortly after Carl Strehlow's time, there is nothing in the Australian literature quite like the Strehlow's early attempts to specify and understand Indigenous ontology (or essence of things).' Years later, Ted and his 'Songs' were to suffer the same marginalisation as his father had, but over time the strength of his values and how they built on his father's pioneering elucidation of spiritual values among the Aranda, became irreversibly established among informed and flexible thinkers. In Clark's view: 'Ted's 'Songs' will grow in importance as other works fade from our canon of prose about Aboriginal culture...The approach [of Songs] and its focus on the subjectivity of Aranda aesthetics, is beyond the purview of more objectivist approaches in anthropology that emphasise social structure, kinship or technology.' The German tradition, in Clark's view, has made its adherents more sensitive to both the means of reflecting inner nature and response to experience.

An interesting aside to the Strehlow story is the formation in the 1930's of a little-known group who called themselves the Jindiworobak Poets. These were Australian poets who valued Ted's influence on Australian writing and sought to 'Indigenise' their own writing. In the words of Rex Ingamells who founded this group: 'Ted had undoubtedly proved just how fertile and imaginative the Aboriginal mind was.'

In 2001, Barry Hill in his 'The Inland Sea', presented a strong case for combining the best of European and Aboriginal values in literature. Now Clark reminds us of how Bruce Chatwin, in his 'Songlines' (1998), paid homage to the way Ted's 'Songs' brought to the nation's attention, perhaps for the first time, the potential of cross-cultural appreciation.

Australia's leading poet Les Murray, probably epitomises, more than any other writer, the influence of Aboriginal values on Australian literature. His widely-acclaimed 'The Human-hair

Thread' clearly acknowledges Ted's deep contribution to Australian identity. Clark surmises that Murray would not have developed into the creative genius which he has become, without the Aboriginal influence so effectively portrayed by the Strehlows. Perhaps like no other poet, Murray has succeeded in giving his Anglo writing an authentic native Australian resonance. This is what Clark refers to as 'a sense of being firmly grounded in a distinctively Australian ecological and social context'. Clark goes on to remind us of how, at the Rotterdam festival some years ago, Murray drew on the Strehlows' insights when he explained the richness, psychological depth and the 'shock' of their portrayal of the dreamtime stories. These attributes, claimed Murray, matched the mythologies of Greece and Rome in their depth of cultural significance and relevance to identity.

Les Murray has been much in the news in recent years and one of the reasons for this, beyond his amazing wordsmithing, is the fundamental way in which his worldview brings the authentic Indigenous view to the Anglo world. As Clark says, 'The potency of such ancestral power is thought to be hidden from everyday view, from the sensory field of waking consciousness, only to be made manifest in dream and ritual.' Both Carl and Ted got this, as did Murray, and they all appreciated how Aborigines' inner lives were connected to and influenced by their ancestral landscape and its totems. The spirituality of this natural grounding, and the land-based religion which reflects it, would have remained hidden from Europeans had not the Strehlows embedded themselves in the Aranda language as no whites had done before.

In hindsight, this essay may be too lavish in its praise of these insightful Lutherans, and perhaps over-critical of the mainstream anthropologists. The fact remains that the Strehlows are owed a national debt, which should rightfully be acknowledged by the Aborigines. Come on Rosalie [Kunoth-Monks], you're a proud Arrernte (Arunta and Aranta) Elder – let's hear it for the Strehlows, who seem to have done more for the recognition and preservation of your Centralian's culture and language than anyone else.

PART FOUR
Australian Identity and Futures

WHAT'S IN A NAME – LIKE MONGREL?

The changing use of names for different 'peoples' which we used to call 'races', is not only a local phenomenon. The well-known 19th century term for natives in Southern Africa originated as the Arabic (Muslim) term for unbelievers or infidels, which was spelled 'caffres' in North Africa. In the United States, the Latin word 'negro' has led to the descriptor 'negroid' referring to the dark skin of the inhabitants of some former Roman colonies. The Latin word 'niger' means 'dark' or 'black'.

In many cases the racial terms were not originally derogatory, but as the relationships between black and white races changed, an understandable effort to change racial names to more respectful alternatives developed. The process often developed as three phases of terminology acceptance:

i.   The first is a long historic period of increasing usage of the original race name.

ii. The second is an increasing awareness among the named people that their commonly used race name carries damaging connotations of inferiority. Often the race name inferred a primitive lack of capacity to operate successfully in the modern world.

iii. The third is a respectful acceptance of new terminology which reflects equality.

The original North American term for a black person was first transformed to 'negro', referring to persons of African slave extraction. In time, the lack of respectability and other negative connotations of 'negro' caused the group concerned to push for acceptance of 'Afro-American' as their collective descriptor. Similarly, Red Indians grew wary of the negative inferences attached to the earlier term 'Redskins'. This led to the contemporary use of 'Amerindians'. In Canada the same thing occurred until the benefits of being called 'Indigenous', or even better, 'First People', caught on in the 1990's.

An unusual case is the Rohinga of Myanmar (Burma) who are regarded by the government as a 'Non-People'; a stateless unrecognised minority of early refugees from the Indian subcontinent. As a non-people, they're not named, not counted and not given the vote. While other minorities campaign for more appropriate names, the Rohinga campaign simply for acknowledgement of their existence.

If we go back far enough in history, we discover that most peoples (nations) were originally referred to by other names. Any cursory study of the origins of today's European and Scandinavian nations, shows how the consolidation of tribes and clans into nation states, led to new group identifiers.

In South Africa the original inhabitants, known for centuries as Bushmen (Boesmans) became recognised as the San People. The coastal Strandlopers (Beach-dwellers) became the Koikoi (or Coloureds under Apartheid) and the Xhosa (Mandela's tribe) and the Zulu (Zuma's tribe) gained the generic name of 'Bantu' which simply means 'people'. The Whites were distinguished as Afrikaners or English-speaking. In Natal and Transvaal, Mahatma Gandhi's people were recorded as 'Indian'. In the Cape, the Asian descendents of slaves of the Dutch were 'Malays', most of whom were Muslim.

It is hard to believe that in this day and age, the Apartheid government were so fiercely intent on preserving the white Afrikaners that laws were enacted to ensure group separation. So, the Mixed Marriage Act 1949, the Immorality Act (1950) and the Population Registration Act (1950) all combined to prevent the mixing of races. In a show of goodwill the government allowed individuals to apply for a change to their official race classification. Taking the Indian example, government statistics show that in 1986 the following numbers of applications were successful:

- Indian to White 4
- Indian to Coloured 63
- Indian to Malay 53

Applications approved to join the Indians were:

- Africans 9
- Coloureds 81
- Malays 43

This bizarre social engineering would have been less traumatic if it applied to whole families, but it didn't because it was mainly based on appearance, a feature which varies greatly between siblings within the same family. The significance of this racial witch-hunt was of course its effect on residential, educational and employment restrictions which differed between race classifications. A serious case in point is the Pageview Indian community near the central business district of Johannesburg, who were forcibly removed to the new Indian township of Lenasia 25 miles away.

In Australia, the natives were first referred to by Captain Cook as 'Indians' – a generic term used by early explorers of the Southern Hemisphere. It was the early anthropologists who promoted the name 'Aboriginal', which was applied worldwide to the native populations of newly discovered lands. This term was used to indicate original inhabitants, whether or not they had a pre-history of migration from Africa, Scandinavia or the Middle East.

Anthropology and archaeology continued to use 'Aboriginal' as a group identifier of this subset of *Homo sapiens* from the early 1800's until the present day. In Australia, several subtypes such as Murrayanas and Barrineans were recognised, all of whom were *Homo sapiens* rather than *Homo erectus*. In recent years there has been an increasing tendency for Aboriginal spokespersons to emphasise the need to replace 'Aboriginal' with a group name which both does away with historical connotations of inferiority, and moves to a new term which highlights prior ownership. So over the past two decades there has been a general shift, first from 'Aboriginal' to 'Indigenous', and more recently from the official-ly-sanctioned 'Indigenous' (as in the Department of Indigenous Affairs) toward the group leadership's preferred term 'First People'. This term is taken from the Canadian Inuit People, who have used it for many years.

The inferences and shades of meaning of group names are of significance, not only to linguists and anthropologists, but also to political movers and shakers. However, the idea that one people were the first to occupy a country, is seen as a meaningful political advantage and bargaining chip, only by a very small minority. Most observers of the racial debate recognise that the historical differences in technological development between peoples, have been the obvious drivers of colonisation. Being first, has seldom been sufficient reason to maintain uncontested land ownership – just ask the Israelis.

The moralists insist that in reality, being first should be

sufficient to claim ownership, and the human rights advocates rely heavily on the undeniable right of first occupation. The Animal Rights advocates, for instance, for African Gorillas or Asian Chimpanzees, hold a very different view to the human righters. Roderick Nash's seminal text titled 'The Rights of Nature' (1989) gives a wonderful legal argument from the US court case on whether trees have 'standing' in preserving them from human destruction. So too, Nash's explanation of the legal arguments which led to the founding of the SPCA in the 1800's. When the 'us and them' arguments move from intra-*Homo* to inter-genera, the assumed pre-eminence of humans starts to look less finite. Since only humans have the vote, the rights of others become academic. It is this Biblical 'dominion over the earth' which initially spawned human arrogance and unleashed global eco-destruction, a process which Indigenes contributed to only in a minor way.

Back in the microcosm of Australian racial politics, the power of martyrism (confected or genuine) continues to tug at the nation's heartstrings, allowing an inherited guilt complex to offer inappropriate racial benefits, which while temporarily assuaging the nation's conscience, has done little to help the original people adapt to the modern world.

History tells us that it takes only one or two great orators to fire up minorities, first to convince themselves that their plight is largely someone else's fault, and second, to further convince them that solidarity through language, culture and land rights, is the only way of consolidating their personal identity and sense of belonging. In the same way, mainstream Australians seek to fabricate a national identity through a combination of wartime patriotism, bush legends and sporting prowess. In developing their unified answer to the 'who are we?' question, there seems to be an ignoring of the fact that as a nation of migrants, we actually don't have the clear homogenous identity which most older nations have.

Some historians have pointed out that with our European history and Asian geography, our sense of belonging in our region is tenuous in the extreme. So when an Asian President warned Australia of becoming the 'Poor White Trash of Asia' if we didn't change our ways, he was really trying to say that while we were in Asia, we weren't of Asia in terms of frugality and humility. His opinion of the Asian-ness of Aborigines is not recorded.

So while Indigenous Australians work hard at consolidating their native pride, they could sympathise with the Whitefellas, many of whom don't seem to know whether they're Arthur or Martha. Both groups would do well to recognise that migration and interbreeding have both contributed to the hybrid vigour (as geneticists call it) of our mixed groups. Seeking the purists archetype of either the Aryan or Aboriginal role model, could be a fruitless and time-wasting exercise in this unique cultural soup of combined gene pools. Pride in being a 'Marvellous Mongrel' has a certain attraction for the independent and self-sufficient inhabitants of this once-Lucky Country. We can leave behind the animal breeders high assessment of purebred stock, and recognise the positive attributes of the mongrel.

My Oxford dictionary tells me that a mongrel is a dog of no definite breed, but also a person 'not of pure race'. Instead of being ashamed of our loss of purity, would it not be inspiring to, (a) appreciate that many pure breeds have both physical and mental shortcomings, and (b) recognise that the practical virtues of mongrels actually outweigh the imagined virtues of the purebreds. It is not necessary to once again exemplify the case of European royal families and the established downside of inbreeding, to make the case for strength in diversity. But it comes at the cost of blurring the concocted image of the iconic national patriot. We'd all do well to just stop this search for 'The Australian', as if a single stereotypical bloke or sheila represented the pinnacle of our racial aspirations. Mongrels can belong, can take pride in their family and can overcome the silly barriers of racial prejudice.

More important than group names are group values, group norms and group priorities. In the best cases they're based on global humanitarian values, many of which are deity-free but firmly based on the Golden Rule.

Let's do it. Let's invite the nation's wordsmiths to come up with an inspiring name for us modern, motivated, moral, mobile mongrels.

Get him Bluey!

WILL THE TRUE PATRIOTS PLEASE STAND UP

In recent years Australia has had a series of self-appointed groups claiming to be the real Australians. By and large, the mainstream haven't taken them too seriously to date, but as these groups proliferate, and as the targets of their hate campaigns move from one minority to another, so their potential to become a serious concern for government increases. So far, there has been no significant public response from government to these far-right fringe-dwellers, although security forces may well have an eye on them.

The Cronulla riots at the end of 2005 exposed an undercurrent of anti-multiculturism, based apparently on both race and religion. In mid 2013 the Party for Freedom held a rally to 'Torpedo the Boats', then in mid 2015 the Reclaim Australia group held a rally which attracted several like-minded groups to combine their allied hates in a show of defiance against a range of minorities – Islamists, Jews, Chinese investors, asylum-seekers, terrorists, 457 visa-holders, non-whites and anyone else who doesn't fit their notion of an Australian patriot.

John Lyons of The Australian (08/08/2015) has produced a very useful piece of journalistic sleuth-work to unpick the contorted world of the far-right. In case we weren't aware, Lyons gives us a short list of organisations which have now thrown their weight behind Reclaim Australia. They include Party for Freedom,

Squadron 88, United Patriots Front, Rise up Australia, Q Society, Golden Dawn, One Nation, Australia First, Australian Defence League, Nationalist Alternative, Patriots Defence League and Restore Australia. Because many members of these rightist groups are not game to identify themselves, a murky anonymous stoush within social media is growing in extent and intensity. Amongst this cadre of haters are the Neo-Nazis who target Muslims and Jews, and who apparently have a habit of infiltrating the more benign groups who just want to stand up for Australian values as they see them, or knew them in the good old days of White Australia. The message from these groups focuses on social media where anonymous hate is easily aired in a cost-free manner which protects the sender's identity.

Matters seemed to come to a head when the Coalition MP George Christiansen addressed a North Queensland rally by Reclaim Australia in mid 2015. He stated that 'there was a good deal of common ground in the political concerns of segments of Reclaim Australia and the concerns of segments of the Liberal National Party (in Queensland)'. When MPs become involved, the debate moves from the social periphery to the political centre. When an MP's office says that there is a 'massive' level of support for Reclaim Australia's ideology, its time for a more significant response from government.

One is reminded of the way in which Hitler emerged as the patriotic champion of the Arian race, the blonde German master-race. It was at the time of the Great Depression and the people needed new hope, new self-esteem and a new goal to strive for; the ideal situation for a Messiah.

Clearly contemporary Australia is not 1930's Germany, but the decision to assess fascism early, is of similar importance. So while it is easy enough, especially in a laid-back trusting society like ours, to dismiss early alarmists as conspiracy theorists who are gullible to imaginary threats, when a dozen like-minded rightists are banding together under one umbrella organisation, the potential threat is heightened.

Let's look again at what it is that bothers these emerging anti-multiculturists. MP George Christiansen's spokesperson is emphatic that he has the guts 'to say what the rest of us are thinking'. Is that true? Perhaps he does speak for a substantial proportion of North Queensland at least. What about the other far-right groups? Do they have legitimate reason to not accept PM Abbott's appeal to 'live and let live'? The United Patriots Front pledges solidarity with Greece's Golden Dawn activists, and no doubt also with the Dutch far-right politician Geert Wilders who wants the Koran banned in his country because it calls on its followers to eliminate the infidels. Wilders was invited to address the Australian Liberty Alliance in Perth, at its launch by the Q Society, a registered anti-Islam political party. Reclaim Australia currently is split, according to Lyons, between those who welcome the Neo-Nazis and those who don't. Squadron 88 takes its name from the eighth letter of the alphabet HH for Heil Hitler, and focuses on anti-Semitism. It appears that this group have found it more acceptable to re-cast themselves as Australian patriots, which brings us back to the basic question: Who are our real patriots?

There are apparently two main subsets within Reclaim Australia, and these are the fundamental Christians and the secular patriots, both preaching exaggerated nationalism. Lyons has been alerted to the real danger of the potential rise of the radical right-wing outside parliament, much like those in Europe, who have developed an increasing current of subterranean discontent, on the basis of both alien philosophy and competition for jobs.

Failure of political leaders to publicly confront these ultra right-wingers may be taken by Reclaim Australia and its satellite groups, as an indication that government may even condone their efforts, notably against radical Muslims. 'It's time for patriotic groups to rise up,' claims Nick Folkes of the Party for Freedom. This party has a Ten Point Plan which is worth summarising here: Stop the invasion by Third Worlders; abolish multiculturism; deport foreign welfare recipients and jail ineligibles; abolish the Human Rights Commission; remove funding from Islamic schools and mosques; deport asylum-seekers; end foreign aid; end 457 visas; restrict foreign property ownership, and promote Australian values and culture through assimilation. It is not clear what proportion of Australians agree with all or some of these tenets, but politicians may be surprised by how significant such support actually is.

A re-consideration of the above Ten Points indicates that there is a smorgasbord of issues to feed intolerance. In fact it caters for all tastes, because many of the points, apart from being racial or religious, are a grab-bag of political choices. It will be interesting to see how our party system handles this emerging ideological focus, whether it's a security threat or not.

FOOTY WAR CRIES – WHATS THE BIG DEAL?

When Adam Goodes did a bit of a simulated spear-throw at the MCG crowd, he set the commentariat off something awful. Trent Dalton has since given a masterly analysis of crowd reaction to this ethnic surprise, but he omitted the historic baggage which goes with War Cries and War Dances such as the internationally renowned Haka of the NZ All Blacks.

It's worth looking again at how War Cries became part of the sporting tradition in the 'great public schools' of Empire. Even the strange expats' performances of the Hash House Harriers, form part of the English propensity to mix tribal ferocity with colonial silliness, so well portrayed in the Monty Python TV series.

The respectful reaction of opposing teams to the Haka, changed some years ago when simulated throat-cutting was added by the Kiwi choreographers. This was a bridge too far and caused some opposing teams to turn their backs. This led to the slitting movement being dropped, leaving the Maori tongue threat as the remaining 'insult'.

For my colonial generation in 1940's South Africa, War Cries were the norm at inter-school rugby matches, as was the raucous singing of rugby songs, complete with pianos heaved up onto the grandstand. In our Border region of the Eastern Cape Province, virtually every boy at our boarding school was descended either from British 1820 settlers or from Boer Trekkers of 1836. Their ancestors had been involved in nine wars with the frontier tribes of the region and they had developed a healthy respect for the inspiring effects of their War Cries. Our first college War Cry was introduced in 1921 when it was in English, using Rugby School's original 'Ra Ra' as its base. Later it was changed to the Xhosa version as still used today. Like the Haka, it was a heartfelt threat to eliminate the opposition (my spelling):

> *Ingunyama!* (We are the lions)
> *Dagabulala!* (We will kill you)
> *Inje, Zimeni, Zintatu* (One, two, three)
> *Zea, Zea, who are we.*
> *QC, QC, yes by gee.*

Looking back, it is hard to fathom how 700 boys in unison, put their heart into such blush-worthy utterances, but that's the way it was. Even without the chest thumping and leg slapping of the All Blacks, when we of the First XV ran out of the tunnel to the thunder from the stand, an ancient warrior pride swelled up within, causing ordinary mortals to rise above their normal selves and tackle like men possessed.

All this must be viewed against a background of a century of inter-racial strife which was much more evenly balanced than the historic Australian situation. The British annexed the Cape for a second time in 1806 and while Treaties, or what the Home Office termed 'Conventions' were made with various tribes, everyone was aware that 'Gunboat Diplomacy' ruled.

Many Anglo-Saxons are probably not really aware of how bellicose their ancestors had been, how picking fights all over the New World was par for the course of Empire. For us boarders of the 1940's, the inclusion of a school armoury containing hundreds of old Snider carbines was nothing remarkable. The history of our Cadet Corp as a force in at least two local battles against the local tribes, was worn as a badge of honour, and our contemporary competition in the British Empire Shield for musketry brought out the best in us Sons of the Veld, whose forebears had lived by the rifle. Both English and Afrikaans-speakers stood tall in the historic reflection of gallantry of the English at Rorke's Drift and the Afrikaners at Blood River. We didn't apologise to anyone for our survival in country which we believed to have been fairly gained by Convention.

When I returned in 2010 to a Reunion of the class of 1950 there was an acceptance by Queen's old-boys, not only that times had changed but that the 80% Black majority at the school could maintain the humanitarian values of our beloved alma mater. The singing of 'N'Kosi Sikilele Afrika' followed by Afrikaans and English verses of 'Die Stem' by the Springboks, had brought home to everyone that equality could flourish. Still, at the reunion of the class of 1950 every old boy could give an inspired rendering of their old Xhosa War Cry as if it was yesterday, to the cheers of their new Black successors in the stand.

So how does this South African national genesis story differ from the Australian scene in which Adam Goodes unwittingly stirred up a hornets' nest at the MCG, an arena which is tribal enough even in the absence of simulated spear-throwing? It all started when Goodes was called an ape by a 13-year-old girl during a previous match. He was justifiably hurt and asked that the perpetrator be identified. He believed his ancestors had actually invented Aussie Rules in its original 'marngrook' form played with a bladder or skin ball. He had mentored the young Indigenous

Flying Boomerangs development squad and had picked up their team War Dance which included warlike gestures to intimidate the 'enemy'. When Goodes took the field again, after yet another classic kick, he instinctively tried his new-found choreography in a one-man challenge to the MCG crowd behind the posts.

So why the fuss causing the commentariat to keep scribing for several weeks? Perhaps, unlike the Rugby crowd who have taken War Cries and Dance in their stride since colonial time, the Aussie Rules mob, with their intense club tribalism have become a bit precious. Dalton has done his homework on crowd behaviour and he quotes an 1800's French 'crowd psychologist' who claimed that, when in a crowd, the individual yields to 'instincts which, had he been alone, he would perforce have kept under restraint. He is no longer himself, no longer conscious of his acts. In the crowd he acts as a barbarian and he possesses the spontaneity, violence and ferocity, the enthusiasm and heroism of primitive beings'.

The Goodes case has both racial and political layers and connotations because here we have a brilliant sportsman displaying his racial pride. His Aboriginal equivalent of 'Log Cabin to White House' success was built on sheer ability and persistence. Until Goodes 'brought racial politics into sport' as his critics claim, he was lauded by all in the same way as they hailed his Black or White footy heroes, one of whom was even referred to as 'God'.

Many AFL supporters, when they refer to Goodes' tribalism, seem unaware of their own tribalism. This is even displayed at old ladies' funerals where their coffins are decked not with the Australian flag but with their beloved club scarves and beanies. How tribal is that?

The stream of press columns on the Goodes saga, from well-known scribes, fight it out in the print media while television and radio shock-jocks play the race card with not-so-subtle jibes in the good-guy/bad-guy assessment of a local-boy-made-good, who cries out for the respect he deserves, but who misjudges the reaction of the fans. Having been nominated for Australian of the Year, he wasn't expecting his show of Indigenous pride to be anything but applauded. The Goodes incident will no doubt be interpreted as a barometer of racial attitudes in this land of the Fair Go for many seasons into the future. What it teaches us is far from clear.

WHEN WE SAY RESPECT, WHAT DO WE MEAN?

Contemporary Australia is trying to come to terms with its history and the present pressures which come from assessing the concept of respect for others. It bursts out in politics, in sport, in education and in health. It is requested, demanded and otherwise expected, but it never seems to properly relate the past to the present. Somehow the 'sins of the fathers' seem to get transferred to the present generation. There is little attempt to recognise that the norms of the past are no longer the norms of the present, nor is there much effort to acknowledge that guilt can't be carried over as an inter-generational black mark. All this applies to both Blacks and Whites in today's Australian population.

In simple terms, this conflicted position aims to divide us into invaders and dispossessed. As an invader, I am being asked to explain myself and justify the immoral behaviour of my original mob. I'm worse than most Australians because I suffer a double-whammy of historic settlement of other people's country. The first was in 1820 when my ancestors were given a block in what was Kaffirland[4] (renamed Kaffraria soon after) in South Africa. It took until 1993 for the Natives to get their land back. I moved my family to Australia in 1975 when racial strife back home was becoming very dangerous. Once in Australia, I was assured by several authors that

---

[4] The term 'Kafir' originally inferred disbeliever or infidel without any derogatory connotation.

I had joined a society which had massacred and dispossessed the country's original owners. Other writers assured me that the same thing had happened to my original ancestors when Britannica was invaded by the Vikings, Romans and Normans, in that order, leaving our Celtish Anglos to adapt or perish under successive new regimes.

Returning to our present identity and discrimination debate, it has become apparent that the 'guilt industry' needs to be given clear time-boundaries, if we're to move forward together. So while ethnic identity has its role in bolstering self-esteem, citizens of a multi-culture have to recognise the rules that we must all play by if we're to benefit from our rich diversity of cultures, norms and behaviours.

Not everyone accepts that respect needs to be earned and is not automatically bestowed on a group or an individual. So saying, 'I'm a proud Arunta man or Anglo man' is okay for self-respect but it should not be expected to necessarily be respected by other ethnic groups. They will judge you on your deeds, your reactions, your contribution, your willingness to not only extend the hand of friendship, but to put your shoulder to the community wheel.

It was good to hear a leading Aboriginal spokesman recently call for an end to the whiteman's guilt, something many of us took for granted because we didn't inherit that mantle. But there is a residual reluctance to put the past behind us, especially by those who prefer to take refuge in martyrism. I have dealt with this matter at length elsewhere (Overcoming Disadvantage 2019) and intend to look ahead without denying the past. It is easier for me, in the present invader class, to air-brush colonial trauma from my attitude to others, while I am fully aware that the tangible effect of dispossession within living memory remain deeply embedded in some of my fellow Australians.

In short, we are faced with a two-sided union: One side needs to offer real equitable opportunities and the other side needs to be given every support to take those opportunities. As a result, the current debate is not about dropping the past racial (that's what it is) baggage, it is about agreeing on ways to move forward together. We must work harder at encouraging the Good Samaritan within us all, we must ensure that our children appreciate that goodness is colour-blind and that kindness is universal. We must shun separatism, we must learn to recognise the virtues of other cultures, to appreciate that there's only one race and that we're in this together. Our futures are tied, and united we can triumph against pettiness, suspicion and rusted-on 'otherness'.

Nice words, I hear you say, but it's not like that in the real world. Perhaps not, but we still need to focus on aspirational goals, which pool our talents, maximise our joint capacity and build the most satisfying foundation for our permanent multiculture. If you are one of those who claims multiculturism isn't working in this country (or the UK or US), ask yourself 'Why?'

Ask yourself whether it's the 'multi' aspect which is inherently fraught or whether it's the lack of will on the part of the participants to reach out, to overcome their unfounded fears, their inbred suspicions and their religious intolerance. There is growing evidence that ethnic groups in many modern countries do not integrate as well as the social engineers had intended, but the reasons for this are conflicted.

In spite of these criticisms, Australia's multiculture is held up as one of the most successful 'migrant' societies, although this rating usually omits the original owner minority. Statistics suggest that migrants make up about 30% of the present population and

Aborigines make up 3%. Several of the migrant groups equate in size to the 500K Aborigines. There appears to be no clear relationship between group size and inter-racial conflict; rather it seems that conflict is related to the extent to which these groups actually integrate socially with the mainstream. In some groups there is a clear range of integration levels among migrant individuals. Depending on personality, many individuals are able to modify their traditionalism to a level which makes them indistinguishable from the mainstream in their lifestyle and behaviour. In many migrant groups there is however, a purist core who insist on strict adherence to their religious and cultural traditions. The same variation can be seen among those who choose to identify as Aboriginal.

There is little that government can do to encourage a richer assimilation, except ensure that minority groups obey the law. However, the populace at large can encourage unity through their own effort to welcome minority groups into community activity and encourage participation.

We should be honest enough to admit that, as a mainstream we haven't always been as welcoming as the minorities might have hoped. This probably applies to most non-English-speaking groups, including rural Aborigines whose communication with others may have suffered from lower education standards.

Somewhere along the integration continuum is an 'ideal' balance between identity and acceptance which reflects a personal trade-off of values. It is widely understood that older migrants find it more difficult to adapt than do their Australian-educated offspring. We also understand the inter-generational stress which this causes within the family. It is often forgotten that no parent actually has the right to insist on the acceptance of their religion or even tradition by their children.

The ideal balance referred to here, is not the only successful societal structure. In fact, many sociologists might argue that, rather than the integrated 'hybrid' multicultural soup described above, a tolerant and co-operative conglomerate of single cultures, can not only satisfy the need for birds of a feather to flock together, but can function as a mini-commonwealth of nations, with each achieving their best within their strongly motivated cultural identity.

One central factor in family identity which is largely overlooked by the more intense religious groups is the UN Rights of the Child. This UN Charter elucidates children's right to choose their own religion and the practices which go with it, when they reach the age of decision-making. Perhaps most parents are unaware that under this Charter, they have a duty to ensure that children have a right to learn about other faiths and to be exposed to alternative philosophies. How these rights conflate family initiations in the parents' faith can be problematic if initiation includes the exclusion of other beliefs. Even the Koran (Quoran) states 'To me, my religion, to you yours,' suggesting a much more tolerant view than the contemporary demand of organisations such as Islamic State. [IS is giving conquered communities three choices; convert to Islam, pay the Infidel financial penalty or face death.]

This pressure to conform to parents tradition is also alive and well among Aboriginal families. The TV program on SBS 'Who we are: Brave New Clan' (15/08/2015) was a well-produced doco on modern, young achievers. Whether each of these impressive role models was asked to mention their tribal pride is not known, but without exception they each indicated how they were defined by their clan and country. Virtually all of these doctors, engineers, artists and musicians had clearly overcome family disadvantage, had grasped the educational opportunity offered, and took pride in their mainstream achievement. They didn't need a special program to empower them, they simply recognised their individual responsibility to reach their potential to contribute.

'I grew up in a very Western lifestyle, but that doesn't make me less Aboriginal', said one of the Sapphires. This reflects a new kind of incipient guilt, the guilt of abandoning your heritage. Nothing wrong with that. 'I must connect to my country, because that's where I get my strength', said another. Don't we all seek our grounding in our family and the places of our formative years? We may ask how different sacred country is to the biblical injunction: 'I will lift up mine eyes to the hills, from whence cometh my help.'

This TV program illustrates we don't need to lose our personal identity to succeed in another lifestyle and set of values. This remarkable selection of young Aborigines all managed to put the concept of 'culturally appropriate' behaviour in a positive and useful context. It allowed them to be truly bi-cultural, drawing on the worlds which they moved between in such a way that ancient grounding complemented modern skills.

In truth, these fine examples of 'getting over it and getting on with it' don't seem to be as tied to traditional ceremony and the reverence of sacred sites, as they are to family and enduring childhood memories. None of them mentioned returning to the Garma or Laura festivals, or the Rainbow Serpent genesis story. Rather they wanted to reward their parents for embracing them with values of education, family bonds and caring.

CULTURAL APPROPRIATION AND CONSTITUTIONAL CHANGE – BIG DEAL?

As objections to the slightest sniff of racism in Australia build up, so any hint that one group have borrowed from another, increasingly becomes a cultural sin. This 'phenomenon of what is termed cultural appropriation' first came to a head in this country when some whitefellas started painting like blackfellas. In the 1960's nobody minded if Albert Namajera painted like whites, in fact he was feted as a great talent and hailed as the new kid on the artistic block.

Throughout history 'primitive' peoples have progressed through the appropriation of others' ideas, behaviour and technology. Virtually all civilisations have been built up this way. This borrowing of good ideas like crop production, domestication of animals, invention of wheels, making of roads, storage of water, building of permanent houses and glazing of pottery, has seen hunter-gatherers like my Druid ancestors, progress from the Stone Age to modern civilisations in all nations except those Indigenous nations who prefer to stagnate rather than step out of their comfort zone of familiar culture.

In Australia offense-taking has become the latest emerging Indigenous art. An example of this is the light-hearted 'Let's Go Walkabout' public festival which had to change its name to 'Let's Go Walkaround'. There are many examples of such cultural silliness which come from Indigenous people whose repeated claim is also that they want to share their culture and knowledge with the mainstream, to enrich the Australian culture. This non-sensical juxtapositioning of culture apparently seems quite appropriate to those cultural over-sensitives whose antennae constantly seek offending behaviour.

How does this backwardness reflect on the mainstream's and government's effort to deliberately offer the benefits of modern western democracy to the keepers of 'precious' First People's values and lifestyle? Firstly, it reflects badly on those parents whose over-emphasis on pride in Indigenous identity, burdens their offspring's transition to modernity. Secondly, this overcooked sense of tribal belonging does nothing to encourage tolerance and adaptation to the needs of the workplace. Thirdly, the sense of separateness and difference, while intended to boost a sense of self-pride and belonging, often has the opposite effect on youngsters who are trying to lift themselves into a position of respect and individual responsibility in the world's most successful multiculture.

Frank Furedi, that keen-eyed social observer from the University of Kent, puts it this way: "Throughout history the most successful societies have been the ones that were open to cultural exchange and borrowing. The most genuine way of respecting another culture is by borrowing and assimilating their achievements." (The Australian 13/2/16)

Surely these words deserve to be writ large in contemporary Australian racial politics. Instead of clarity and detailed solutions proposed to correct present inequities in Australia, we have prime ministerial rhetoric which speaks of a bright future for all, despite the patchy progress in 'Closing the Gap', a concept first mooted in 2006 under PM Howard and embraced by Kevin 07 in his Apology to the Stolen Generation in 2008.

The most recent statement on Aboriginal progress was made by PM Turnbull in February 2016. He was realistic about shortcomings on the latest Gap report but he avoided contentions issues such as a Treaty, Self-government or (heaven forbid) Sovereignty. Frustration is running at an all-time high among Aboriginal leaders whose attempts to devise, submit and debate pragmatic solutions to empower their people, have so far been met with silence, even after a full year of receiving the most comprehensive report on practical empowerment of Indigenous communities.

Instead of trying to correct past inequities through constitutional change, a comprehensive Treaty could finally clarify precisely how government and Indigenous people view Aboriginal Futures. It has been decades since anyone in government offered an explanation of why a Treaty is inappropriate, unworkable or illegal. Meanwhile Australia could be staring a failed Referendum on Recognition in the face, while a simple wording-change recognising three major waves of population growth, of which First People were the originals, could fix the demand for recognition. If the word 'race' requires removal, a simple rewording (or elimination) of Sections 25, 51 and 127 could meet non-racial requirements. However, the Constitution is no place for spelling out the details of rights and non-discrimination. A Treaty however, could do this in a way which is at least as equally inviolable as constitutional wording could.

While all this brouhaha about the Constitution contrives to fill the daily press, two other issues are treated by the public as though they are someone else's business: incarceration rates and child removal. Both these matters reflect badly on our society. The former has exercised the minds of jurisdictions for many years without a workable solution being offered. The latter is now so desperate that the case is being driven by 'Grandmothers Against Removal'. Officialdom gives three reasons for child-removal: violence and abuse, poverty, and parent's incapacity to provide a safe environment for child-rearing. This issue is a very good example of why constitutional change is unlikely to affect well-being. At the same time, the grandmothers point out that the parents are not responsible for the poverty and depravation that their families suffer. At this point the responsibility argument comes full-circle and the blame-game re-ignites the argument about the deep and ongoing effects of dispossession on a powerless people.

Constitutional changes, Treaties, Bills of Rights or Legal Equity will mean nothing in terms of well-being until the people themselves recognise and accept that without individual and group initiative to seek and use opportunities, no amount of legislative support can empower the people. It is not the law which oppresses or frees people; rather it is mature personal responsibility which drives corrective action. It is the absence of applying what Pearson many years ago called 'the Right to Take Responsibility' which now holds the key to equality and thus demands national priorities.

DON'T MENTION
THE TREATY

Australia has voluminous national literature on the subject of a Treaty between Aborigines and the federal government. The somewhat tiresome list of reasons why the mainstream believe that a Treaty is not a good idea has never been seriously tested in a logical forum of legal specialists.

Every decade or so, the Treaty idea gets a brief airing, then disappears once more into oblivion. Today, with the focus on Indigenous recognition in the Constitution, the Treaty lobby recognises a rare window of opportunity to do one of two things:

i.   Use constitutional change to embed Indigenous recognition so unambiguously into the Constitution that a Treaty becomes an automatic sequitur to recognition, or

ii. Insist that constitutional recognition will be a sell-out of substantial Indigenous interest, which would be used to dismiss future Treaty demands as irrelevant.

Both these stances by opposing factions within the Aboriginal community, offer what are claimed to be well-founded legal argument for their cause.

Most informed commentators probably recognise that the number of unknowns in the Constitution and/or Treaty debate, make it impossible to pre-judge the outcomes. Whether or not constitutional change helps or hinders a Treaty; it is beyond high time that mainstream Australians had a more enlightened appreciation of what a Treaty might imply.

For about 15 years ATSIC had, through its National Treaty Support Group (NTSG), promulgated the benefits of a Treaty, at least for Aborigines. This group maintain that a Treaty could simply be a contract, or enacted by legislation, or arise from constitutional change, or it could even be enacted under International Law at Geneva, the Hague or the United Nations.

It is often pointed out that Canada, U.S. and New Zealand all offer practical examples of workable Treaties, so what's so different about Australia? Historically what's different is that in Australia the Indigenes never offered any serious organised resistance to the invaders. All three of the above countries were colonised by Britain and the record of first contact tells us that Britain only found it necessary to sign Treaties or Conventions when she couldn't get away with her good old unilateral Annexation.

This well-tried mechanism of sovereignty simply stated that the new land was claimed in the name of the reigning monarch. The Indigenes opinion was irrelevant and never sought. So why should it be sought now, in a world which inherited the 'might is right' view of land ownership?

The Treaty advocates are not put off and repeatedly point out that a modern Treaty would enable Australia to gain at least five 'advantages':

i.   It allows the formalisation of relationships between Indigenous and non-Indigenous Australians.

ii. It gives the nation the opportunity to redress past wrongs.

iii. It provides a mechanism for protecting Indigenous rights.

iv. It provides a platform on which unfinished currencies of equity and compensation may be determined.

v. It offers a framework for self-determination and political freedom.

It is on the voracity of these claims that the case for a Treaty would stand or fall. Those who have tried to make a legally-binding case for a Treaty on the above grounds have found more than a little opposition to their case and as a result, the Treaty case has almost always reverted to being dealt with as a moral and humanitarian issue. Invariably government points out that contemporary standards and norms cannot simply be applied retrospectively to a 200 year time-lapse. Once again the dominant culture reminds us that historically most nations were invaded, in fact many were invaded several times over, as was the case with the British before they became the United Kingdom.

The Treaty proponents state that, irrespective of past waves of colonisation, contemporary Australia still lacks a clear and agreed basis for the negotiation of a range of well-being issues which currently disadvantage Aborigines. These include the prohibition of discrimination, access to education, training and employment, recognition of tribal and clan identities, justice and legal standing, settlement for the Stolen Generation, control of land and water management and financial reparations. The government in turn, believes that most of these matters have in fact been attended to.

The Treaty advocates are at pains to emphasise that unless they can negotiate a legally enforceable Treaty, they're wasting their time. In addition, the wording of the Treaty and its explanatory notes will need to be unambiguous to avoid unforeseen interpretations by the courts which may disadvantage Aboriginal aspirations.

These Treaty advocates emphasise that the objectives and spirit or intentions of the Treaty are of critical importance, as was the case in New Zealand. In this sense, the intent of the Treaty must be adjudicated as a binding contract and as such, must be interpreted under Contract Law. The Treaty is also seen as being constitutionally protected, i.e. its intent must also be clear in the wording of the Federal Constitution. Failing acceptance by the Commonwealth, the Treaty must be upheld by an International Treaty and interpreted under the rules of International Law.

Constitutional lawyers assure us that a Treaty agreed upon by contract or legislative approval would not require any change to the Constitution and would not require a Treaty Referendum. However, Treaty negotiations would need to include agreement on the structure and process of Treaty administration. It has been proposed that a Treaty Commission could be established, similar to the NZ Waitangi Tribunal of the 1970's or the Treaty Commission in Canada's British Columbia in1990. In the BC case, the Commission was established prior to Treaty negotiations, so that it could ensure a solid basis for the Treaty and its implementation.

Whether there are advantages to the Treaty Commission being independent of both negotiating parties would require prior agreement, as would the nomination rules for such a body. This brings the debate to the long list of questions which have never been properly answered by any Federal government. It is worth the nation considering each of these, because without an understanding of the implications of a Treaty for each of these issues, voters will not know what they're actually voting for in a Treaty Plebiscite or Referendum.

Only a few cardinal questions are dealt with here, but they illustrate the seminal nature of a range of issues. For instance, is it true that only sovereign nations can sign Treaties? Will citizens of each have different rights? Is citizenship affected, and if so, how? Is it not, as many have suggested, too late to enter into a Treaty? Apart from the perceived endorsement of Aboriginal rights and advantages, what unplanned outcomes could a Treaty bring for the majority?

The central question of whether Aborigines would cede their sovereignty to the Commonwealth under a Treaty, remains a crucial issue. The capacity of a People to exercise self-government under a Treaty which allows self-determination is a strongly-held aspiration of most Treaty proponents. The fact that Aborigines never gave up their sovereignty or ceded their territory to the invaders, is held up as the prime reason why Aborigines feel justified on insisting that they remain a sovereign nation of First Peoples.

They maintain that, just as Native Title was favoured by the High Court, never to have been extinguished by colonial land titles, so Aboriginal sovereignty also remains, having never been ceded. In this way their legal argument remains one of extant original ownership and land rights. The fact that the Commonwealth has never recognised their law or nationhood does not, in their view, diminish the status of their everlasting original rights.

It's about time the Treaty debate was seriously pursued in the public square – now[5], not after the Constitutional Referendum.

---

[5] The most recent (30/7/16) feedback from regional referendum council meetings indicates a strong preference for Treaties with each major language group – as proposed by Michael Mansell for his provisional Aboriginal Government in Central Australia two decades ago.

TRADING TRADITION FOR WELL-BEING

The Broad Choices

For twenty-five years I have studied the possibility of Aborigines becoming fully integrated into mainstream Australia, where their full potential can be achieved, appreciated and built on alongside the rest of the population.

My conclusion to date, is that two prime factors mitigate against early achievement of this position:

i. A less than welcoming reception into the body of the nation by the Anglo and Migrant subcultures.

ii. The increasing insistence by the Aboriginal activists to remain a separately identified group, desirous of maintaining not only tribal identity, but also custom, tradition, ceremony and Dreamtime values as the foundation for a potentially sovereign nation of First Peoples.

Of course, there are many exceptions in both population groups and my conclusion can be easily gainsaid by the quoting of numerous personal examples. That said, the great divide in willingness to adapt to Western humanitarianism among many Aborigines, and willingness to accept Aborigines among non-Aboriginals, both appear to loom large as co-contributors to a significant resistance to integration. As a result, 'integration' is a dirty word to Aboriginal traditionalists.

Let's look at the stereotypical arguments for and against integration by Aborigines:

One

First there is the well-worn white view that, 'We are not racists, but Aborigines can't be expected to be welcomed into the fold of the mainstream, unless they change their ways and live by modern humanitarian norms.' The usual suspects, who put forward this view, generally have no understanding of the background to why Aborigines live and behave the way they do. They're simply classed as primitive and unready for modern society.

It is noteworthy that this view is not limited to the Anglo segment of Australia's population but reflected, perhaps even more blatantly, among both European and Asian migrant business people. To this extent, anti-Aboriginal discrimination cannot be linked only to the colonising British, but reflects a more global form of reaction to 'The Other'. This concept of 'otherness' has been much-studied by sociologists and psychologists and is apparently seen primarily as a fear factor – fear of the unknown. In practice this fear exhibits rather as disdain and rejection, from which various forms of disrespect, even offensive behaviour, develops.

Many studies have shown that, while personal racism is always denied, skin colour and some facial features, have been demonstrated to play a major role in the appointment of job applicants. Australian, American and European research supports the conclusion that such race-based discrimination is not just a historical fact in Western society, but is alive and well in many modern societies.

The good news is that this tendency to appoint staff 'who are like us', is decreasing, albeit slowly. One study proved that approximately 30% of the bias against Africans, Afro-Americans and other dark Indigenes, cannot be explained by inadequate qualifications or lack of experience.

Two

The second position, is the Aboriginal response to what they see as non-acceptance, even rejection, by many in the mainstream. Their response goes something like this: Many of our mothers and most of our nannas, instilled in us the need for an education such as many of them had had, at least in rudimentary form, on the missions and reserves. Many of our old folks took on Christian values which augmented our traditional equivalent of the Good Samaritan and Doing unto Others. Those of us who had the inner strength to resist the peer pressure to drink and steal, did try to develop trade skills so we could join the workforce and support our long-suffering mothers. But somehow the jobs seldom came our way, especially when the mainstream unemployment rate rose above 5%.

Three

There is a third response to the invitation to integrate and benefit from mainstream well-being. This response is more ideological than the first two responses, and it is the conviction that the only way Aborigines can be sure of respect and real pragmatic equality, is to pursue a separate nationhood by Treaty or Sovereignty or both.

Such separatism has been seen as ill-advised, constitutionally untenable and plainly impractical by successive Federal governments, but it is an aspirational goal held firmly by a large number of both activists and leaders who believe that they carry the imprimatur of their First People.

The models of a 'Sovereign Aboriginalia' which have been proposed to date, not only lack operational detail but are geographically vague. This is not to say a new sovereignty could not be constructed, given sufficient political will, but a considerably more credible vision of the new entity will be required before it can be expected to be taken seriously by the government and the mainstream.

Enter Stan Grant

As one of those who have been forging our views of Aboriginal futures, NITV anchorman of the Awaken programme, is not usually referred to in the same breath as the established Aboriginal leaders such as Langton, Dodson, Pearson or Mundine. But Stan Grant, like Pearson, brings a wealth of media experience to his job of convening regular Aboriginal panel discussions under the Awaken banner. As an opinion-maker rather than a king-maker, Grant manages his questions to panellists in a professional and diplomatic way. He deliberately avoids the 'attack dog' interviewer style of the local Radio Shock Jocks, and that's understandable, given his task of building the image of Aboriginality and nurturing the confidence of his brothers and sisters on the panel.

In both his speaking and his writing, Grant impresses with his mature reasonableness. However to those of us wanting him to challenge the frequent naive and unprogressive views of many of his older interviewees, Grant keeps failing to ask the hard questions and challenge the answers he's given. The considerable personal baggage which Grant carries, as exposed in an interview by Victoria Laurie in the Weekend Australian magazine (14/11/15), puts him in a somewhat delicate position as a campaigner for the Aboriginal cause. He speaks fondly of his White maternal grandmother but would apparently rather not answer questions on his early attempts to be White.

With 16 years of experience of overseas reporting and being now married to a well-known broadcaster, Grant walks a racial tightrope with a finesse which belies what many viewers probably consider to be his actual experiential conviction on the best way forward, i.e. adaptation and unity.

Grants interviews with notable Aborigines like Ernie Dingo and Mark Ella, reflect an easy-going acknowledgement of the personal well-being which stems from real talent and mainstream participation. But when he states how appalling it is that a Treaty and Sovereignty aren't even on the table for public discussion, Grant reflects his NITV role-expectations. He accuses, quite rightly in my view, Australia of not tackling these basic issues in the way that several other countries have – years ago.

Some of us remember the younger Stan Grant as an international reporter. That he was an Aboriginal never crossed our minds then. He was an Australian doing a great job in the global media. Unbeknown to us was the discrimination and hurt he had suffered in his youth. When asked about Australia as a racist society, Grant was adamant: 'Australia has racism at its foundation. The idea of *terra nullius* justified the theft of our land. The Constitution has race provisions that have, at times been used for [making] laws that took children, stopped us voting, told us where we could live or who we could marry...we've never been empowered to determine our destiny as a people. Australia is a remarkable country, but it has a stain on its soul and my people have paid a terrible price for Australia's prosperity.'

To Grant's credit, it must be acknowledged that his 'Awaken' program is the only hour of NITV's daily offerings which achieves any depth of mature debate on Aboriginal policy and future direction. Grant must also be credited for often acting as Devil's Advocate, asking the relatively hard questions, but in a soft way.

However, he too often lets his guests get away with ill-founded statements on policy and culture, which do nothing to help his mob cope with the modern world. In addition, his support for adaptive modernity is often weaker than would normally be required from a potential role model for his people. The NITV program schedule is in serious need of an adult in-depth contest of ideas. Its sport, children's programs, traditional stories and outside broadcasts are generally well produced and useful as building blocks for Aboriginal identity and culture, but its equivalent of 'Q&A', '7.30' or 'Lateline' is missing. The closest to these ABC mainstream programs is SBS's 'Insight', so excellently presented by Jenny Brocky.

Brocky invariably has a multiracial studio audience, but unlike 'Q&A', she asks the questions and encourages conflicting views. Aboriginal voices make only a minor contribution to her debates and she always insists on including opposing views on the topic of the day. Grant would do well to consider offering 'Awaken' in the format of 'The Drum', focussing on topical events affecting Aborigines but deliberately seeking guests of diverse views, rather than the all-too stereotyped personalities he currently invites in. Grant seems to see his role as strengthening Aboriginality not testing validity of its proponents' logic.

The comparison of the NITV and SBS charters probably indicates somewhat overlapping missions and goals. SBS is considerably older than NITV and was established to serve the radio and television needs of Australia's migrant groups. With broadcasts in every language from Urdu to Swahili, SBS usually only deals tangentially with Aboriginal issues, but as a global leader in multiculturalism it is to be heralded as an unusually inclusive broadcaster. However, many taxpayers have asked why the context of NITV could not have been included in SBS's brief. The answer is that the client group of NITV is different, original, historically oppressed and politically significant, even if their numbers are no greater than several migrant groups.

So those of us in the public square, patiently waiting for an official decision on separatism by whatever name, see those traditionalists who continue to insist that their clan identity should forever continue to define themselves, as holding back productive unity for the rest. So who should call the shots in this minority decision? Noel Pearson's outstanding piece in the Quarterly Review (issue 55, 2014), titled 'A Rightful Place', probably does more to answer this question than any other writing.

When Will Child-Wellbeing Trump Cultural Appropriateness?

If there is one thing that gets us contemporary humanitarians going its child abuse. We see it in many forms: sexual abuse by religious organisations, domestic violence against children, abuse of children in refugee camps, trafficking of girls by Islamist radicals, and child labour in Asia. Our Western Christianity has probably inculcated a resilient inheritance of the original 'suffer the little children' concept in us post-Christian secularists.

In the Australian situation, this concern for children has additional historic connotations resulting from the missionary zeal of the churches' and the government's commitments to saving young people from what they considered barbarity. As educated, enlightened and Christian 'Bringers of the Light', they saw the passing generational pain of child loss as a small price to pay for 'rescuing' these children from primitive darkness.

That was until the Australian Human Rights Commission in 1996 produced its Stolen Generation Report entitled 'Bringing Them Home'. The range of human emotions that were also reflected in Dorothy Pilkington's 'Rabbit Proof Fence' film, graphically reminded mainstream Australians of the Indigenous views of child removal. Seen through the eyes of Gracie and her siblings as they battle their way home over 1000 kilometres of stony country to Jigalong, following the world's longest fence, only the hardest of hearts could not empathise with their plight. Few would be unmoved by the film or the report, but times have moved on to the present era, where the new focus is on domestic violence which has reached such proportions in this country that special task forces have been set up to counter this scourge of contemporary Australia, both Black and White.

In simple terms, we have a social issue of plague proportions in which wives and children are eventually forced to leave home for their own safety. A subset of this heart-rending situation is the question of removing children from violent homes, notably Aboriginal children whose statistical likelihood of being physically, sexually and mentally abused, is orders of magnitude greater than in other population groups.

What has happened during the past decade is that Australia's social workers have increasingly been challenged to favour, not family unity, but individual child well-being. In the process, media personalities and radio shock-jocks have had a field-day giving tear-jerking accounts of removed children, damaged non-removed children, and families torn apart by what is seen as today's Stolen Generation. This hype likes to use the phrase 'ripped from their mother's arms' even when there is a clear benefit to the child.

Of course there are two sides to the child-removal issue, but this particular debate must be seen as an important subset of the Indigenous Futures national conversation. This conversation centres on the need for individual responsibility as the central and essential element, without which respect and real equity can never be attained. This is what Noel Pearson called 'The Right to Take Responsibility' more than a decade ago.

One of the problems which cause social workers and their political masters to follow the humanitarian sentiments of 'Bringing Them Home', is that this view is so politically delicate and the family unit repeatly overrides the right of the child. The pundits suggest that removing the perpetrators is obviously preferable to removing the victims. They add that this principle is colour-blind, although percentage-wise it would affect Indigenous families more often than others. The focus on 'culturally appropriate' social policy adds a significant factor to official decision-making on child protection.

No consideration of the realities of child removal is complete without examination of the case study of Kia Shillingsworth. Kia was a four-year-old Aboriginal whose abuse in her home eventually ended in her death at the Murray-Darling town of Brewarrina. Despite efforts to save Kia, the accumulated effects of several medical conditions finally took her short life in 2012. It is now 2016 and the call for cultural awareness is still loud in the land, but in the public square the people are calling for clarity on what this culture, which they are asked to be aware of, actually stands for. To what extent does it reflect traditional and ancient values and mores? Are these cultural behaviours not only appropriate to its values, but also appropriate to a modern multicultural nation? How is national unity and social cohesion viewed by this apparently separatist culture?

With these questions in mind, little Kia's rights loom large. The coroner in her case wrote that Kia died, like too many others in remote Aboriginal communities, of the disease of poverty at an early age. Jeremy Sammut (The Australian 20/2/16) reminds us that the NSW Department of Family and Community Services received several reports highlighting social workers' concerns for Kia's well-being. These reports were not unusual in recording physical and medical neglect, overcrowding and inadequate supervision. A combination of infections was reported as causing her death by rheumatic heart disease. Clearly Kia died from neglect despite the fact that the family stated to the social worker that she was healthy, happy and active.

Sammut advises us that even after reviewing four increasingly urgent reports about neglect of children at Kia's home, the Department still didn't investigate. There was also considerable evidence in remote communities of social worker desensitisation as a result of the extent of the normalisation of neglect. Nobody believes that such abandoning of humanitarian standards by professionally-trained social workers would have occurred without political pressure from government to not remove children if at all possible. The voting public still awaits inside information about directives to field staff on child removal criteria and aspirational numbers. It would be unsurprising if such detailed instructions were never recorded or available for public scrutiny under Freedom of Information.

It is one thing for Aborigines to repeat claims that Non-Indigenous mainstreamers would never understand their worldview and the values and behaviours which stem from their culture. It is quite another thing to demand that out-dated social norms be accepted as appropriate for modern child-rearing. The additional claim that Aboriginal family life was peaceful, harmonious and non-violent in pre-colonial days and that violence is the result of dispossession, is more than simplistic. It is high time that Aboriginal activists stopped pretending that their ancient culture warrants acclaim and respect by others solely because of its antiquity and earth-friendly activities.

Sammut reminds us that the Special Commission of Inquiry into Child Protection Services in New South Wales (Wood Report) warned that mainstream social workers 'may find it difficult to understand the complexity of Aboriginal family and kinship relations...' That may well be true, as might the parents' view on where their children should live if home is unsafe. What is not true, is the claim that 'sacred' family unity overrides child safety.

This matter is comprehensively dealt with in the book 'The Madness of Australian Child Protection' (Sammut 2015) which persuasively argues the case for adoption but probably doesn't make a strong enough case on why White mainstream adoption could be at least as effective in nurturing healthy, well-adjusted Indigenous children.

So the question remains: When will Aboriginal activists put child well-being above cultural appropriateness? Before constitutional change we hope.

Note: Since writing this essay, Grant has published his life story 'Talking to My Country' and now compares the nightly interview show 'The Point' on NITV.

PART FIVE

Pearson and The Constitution

PEARSON –
LONE RANGER

The past few years have seen a number of bodies and individuals give their opinion on how Aborigines should be recognised in Australia's Constitution. Noel Pearson of Cape York Partnerships, has been an important player, not only in this recognition process, but in advising Governments for the past two decades.

By the present advanced stage of debate on constitutional recognition, while many observers are commenting on the increasing number of progressive opportunities, Pearson has been making new and possibly conflicting inputs into the recognition process. As a lawyer, he has always been active in encouraging government to change policy to allow Aborigines to join mainstream socio-economic wealth-generation, but has never beaten the sovereignty drum or espoused the separatist tradition. In fact, the index of his collected papers, 'Up from The Mission', doesn't mention the words sovereignty, independence or self-government.

Pearson was a member of the multi-million dollar Expert Panel which recommended to government how recognition in the Constitution could best be achieved. If he held views different from the Panel's recommendations, it must be assumed that he failed to push them, or if he did, he failed to convince the Panel. Either way, the Panel's recommendations are very different from the proposal Pearson made in his Cape York Institute's (CYI) submission. The

CYI proposed a new Act protecting language and a second Act to establish an Aboriginal advisory body to Parliament.

At least a year later Pearson came up with a third proposal based on his belief that radical change to the Constitution would not pass a referendum. His proposal was to avoid conflict with constitutional conspiracy theorists who saw recognition as a disguised Bill of Rights. This, he suggested could be overcome by simply adding a generously-worded adjunct document on recognition to be read alongside the Constitution.

This third input of Pearson's arose from ideas suggested by two Jewish lawyers who proposed a way of sidestepping the Constitution while making an even more comprehensive, even poetic, statement on the position of Aborigines within the national legal framework.

When commentators suggested that, as a Panel member, it was inappropriate for Pearson to keep making multiple new proposals, Pearson reminded them that the Recognition office was receiving proposals right up to 30 June 2015 and that there were no limits on an individual's proposals, provided they were relevant.

Then, just when we thought Pearson had done his dash on constitutional proposals, he came up with something no Aboriginal had ever done before – he strongly recommended that white Australians cease their guilt and put an end to silly policy based on nothing more than pretending to rectify historic wrongs by offering more welfare, more special treatment, more disincentive for Aborigines to take responsibility for their actions, and more undeserved financial assistance with passive welfare, special education payments and racially-based business loans. Pearson's call for the end of the 'guilt industry' should have come from Aboriginal spokespersons thirty years ago. Why didn't it? Because they were benefitting big time and in a double-barrelled way. Firstly, the make-work employment schemes for dole payment were manna from heaven (or from Kevin). Secondly, the psychological warmth which flowed from the never-ending martyrism, fed by the guilt-trip, perpetuated the comforting feeling of the self-oppressed that their condition was largely someone else's fault.

No wonder Pearson's concept of the guiltless whitefella went down like a lead balloon with the full-time activists and what Pearson calls 'the campaign Aborigines' whose entire reason for being, depends on thumping the oppression drum. No guilt, no *raison d'être* for the professional banner-carriers and flag-burners.

So here we have the most complex and astute racial commentator, acting very much as the Lone Ranger, seldom in a team unless he's captain, and able to cause waves with radical ideas dropped into the political pool, seemingly at random but actually well-planned. His complexity has several facets, two of which are the juxtaposed deep-thinking intellectual whose mastery of English and exceptional articulation, put him in a class of his own, and the rude bully-boy whose coarse language and personal abuse of white bureaucrats and politicians, are difficult to reconcile. Another axis of his complexity is the way his altruistic pendulum swings between tear-jerking stories of Elders and untrammelled praise for white heroes who have inspired him; among the latter are: the American linguist who mastered his Hopevale mother-tongue; the Lutheran missionaries who stood up for Pearson's people against the State government; and the Jewish lawyers where he did his Articles and learned a new tribal pride and identity.

Another axis of his complexity, is Pearson's grasp of the Left-Right nexus in Australian politics and his understanding of the weird factions within Labour, which are often no more than personality-cults without even a smidgeon of difference in principle or ideology. Yet another contrast in this unique personality, is his personal double-life of the city-slicker, perfectly adapted to modern Western ways, who repeatedly feels the call of the bush, the pull of clan country, the grounding experiences of a natural childhood, before he morphed into his contemporary bi-cultural self.

We can only conclude that Pearson is unique and stands head and shoulders above his mob. Pleasing them all is another matter, one he has yet to master.

VALUING ABORIGINALITY THE PEARSON WAY

The contrasted Three Cheers view and the Black Armband view of Australian racial history have yet to be reconciled. Both camps believe their values and the policy logic which flows from them, are not only rational but justifiable.

The process of finding an acceptable way of formally recognising Aborigines (Indigenous or First People) has given Australians a special opportunity to analyse and weigh up their perceived truths in race relations. Perhaps the most incisive consideration of the issues at stake in this process, is the unusually well-researched submission by Noel Pearson and his legal researcher, Shireen Morris, on behalf of the Cape York Institute in September 2011. As far as I can make out, this document of experience and research, stands alone in the realm of what I'd call race rationale, and as such, it warrants serious critique of its claims and proposals. Having studied Pearson's magisterial writings for many years and having held several meetings with Morris at their Cairns office, it may be appropriate to offer an in-depth analysis of at least one section of their substantive submission, using their own *statements*. This is most logically done by following their quotations with my response.

Some of the terminology in the responses may be regarded as disrespectful or even arrogant by some of our culturally-appropriate colleagues. In assessing the logic and rationale of the ideas put forward here it will help if the reader tempers any precious outrage, with the expected open-mindedness of the genuine scholar when seeking truth.

One

'Of the many problems Australia still faces with regards to Indigenous affairs, two problems are of utmost importance: One, Indigenous Australians still suffer disproportionate levels of poverty... Two, Indigenous cultures and languages continue to disappear ... Indigenous Australian culture is a suppressed part of our Australian identity.'

I agree with the factual correctness of both these statements, but whether they are of 'utmost importance' to the other 97% of the population is unlikely. Whether they should be, is another question. Australians are generally ambiguous about embracing Aboriginal culture as part of themselves, although in the absence of unanimity on an alternative national identity (apart from the Anzac tradition) there is an undeclared attraction of grounding in the country itself, as Aborigines do.

Two

'Why hasn't the Constitution enabled Indigenous socio-economic and cultural prosperity and equality within Australia? The answer is, because it was not intended to. It was drafted deliberately excluding and ignoring Indigenous Australians. It was born from a colonial system and has perpetuated colonial myths of Indigenous Australian inferiority, dependency and incapability.'

This statement is essentially correct but the reasons for exclusion at the time of Federation deserve closer scrutiny. There seems to be a denial of the realities of how the differences in advancement between peoples naturally lead to the more progressive peoples (cultures, civilisations, technologies) to go searching for greater resources. This is the history of the world, based not on empathy or fairness, but rather on strength of organisation and technology. So while Indigenous (we were here first) peoples value their own identity, their expectation that others will similarly value their culture, stretches the understanding of human nature beyond credence. However, the 'that's just how it was in those days' justification for exclusionary policies, is insufficient for modern humanitarianism.

Answering the historic question of whether Aborigines of the contact era were in fact 'inferior and incapable', depends on how hunter-gather capabilities were viewed in the emerging capitalist production system. While Aboriginal knowledge of nature was without peer, it had limited application to the new occupations of agriculture and mining. It was in that context that the superiority and capability of the newcomers must be conceded, although this in no way diminishes the fact that these industries have eroded and salinised vast areas, in addition to diminishing biodiversity, as described in the book 'Sustainable Agriculture and Land Use' (Roberts 1995).

Three

'Australia has never yet put in place mechanisms or guarantees to ensure the realisation of equal rights and responsibilities for Indigenous Australians.'

This is true when 'rights and responsibilities' are considered as one conplimentary entity, but the real question is: Has Australia guaranteed equal rights and responsibilities to other citizens, including migrants from 93 countries of origin? The answer is probably 'yes', given the wording of the Australian citizenship declaration, read and agreed to by all newcomers. There is only so much that government can put in place policy-wise, the rest is up to the individual – learn the language of industry, acquire the skills for employment, invest the income wisely, contribute to national income, respect universal norms of social cohesion and accept the criteria of good Australian citizenship. There is little doubt that the mainstream would welcome a greater effort by Aborigines to become self-starters and responsible contributors to our productive capitalist democracy. Whether they are correct in their estimation of the extent to which Aborigines' historic, inherited, inter-generational disadvantage prevents them, physically and mentally, from joining the competitive workforce warrants serious consideration. The Right wing suggest that this historic excuse has reached its use-by date and has become an invalid martyristic attempt to avoid modern reality and to retreat into the 'comfortable' refuge of post-colonial trauma. Exaggerated Indigenous identity has become so precious as to override any requirement to get real about participation in the productive humanitarian mainstream.

Four

'Indigenous Australian cultures and languages must finally be celebrated as an indispensable part of Australian identity. They must be supported to prosper and to be enjoyed by the whole nation…'

No doubt Indigenous culture can and does enrich Australian life, however there are no clear-cut answers to the valuing of culture.

Whether ancient tradition is regarded as indispensable by the Australian mainstream is most unlikely. Interesting, yes. Ancient, yes. Essential, probably not. Historic rock-art is very different from acrylic commercial dot-painting on masonite. Authentic Indigenous music is very basic and usually not attractive to the mainstream. Languages may be interesting to linguists but their usefulness to modern Australia is limited to a small group. This is not to gainsay the emotive connection to mother-tongue language, as demonstrated by many nations whose identity is closely aligned to 'tribal' language, be it Aboriginal, Welsh, Yiddish, Gaelic, Indian, Afrikaans or Chinese. The extent to which they must be 'supported to prosper' (by the taxpayer) is far from agreed. Why would Aboriginal language be funded beyond Greek, Italian, Hebrew, Arabic and Afrikaans, particularly when the size of these migrant populations approximate the Aboriginal population?

Linguists prefer to avoid the 'usefulness' criterion in their appreciation of languages, so while there may be a case for using both English and Aboriginal place-names, convincing the mainstream of the priority of school-time on fluency in Aboriginal language is probably a battle lost, compared to alternative curriculum content. At the same time, Aborigines should be encouraged to extend their languages within their communities' cultural societies. Others in the mainstream will have grounds to disagree with this stance, and could make a persuasive case for their acceptance of Pearson's and Morris' insistence on the 'indispensability' of their preferred culture to the rest of Australia.

Five

'Closing the Gap' is to be achieved by expecting more of Australians, not less; by listening more, not ignoring them. We must start by

admitting the errors we have made in our history. There has been
too much adverse discrimination against Indigenous Australians.
More recently there has been too much 'positive' discrimination with
adverse results, driven by White guilt and perpetuating Indigenous
Australian victimhood. The 'soft bigotry of low expectations' lingers
on.'

It is true that expecting more from Aborigines is the way to go, but while the 'you can do anything' motivation by teachers, such as Chris Sarra, may resonate with a limited number of young people whose 'readiness' is high, it may only end in tears for the rest, who find it just not realistic for them. The 'more' must become a new norm, starting with 'doing nothing' and moving to 'doing something' useful for self and society. For the more capable individuals it may progress to 'doing something really useful' and in the process, becoming a valued and respected member of society. This is not a sprint but a marathon, and forcing the pace, understandable as this is for the urgent mentors, could set personal progress back years.

As for 'listening more and ignoring less', this clearly needs to be a two-way process. The Aboriginal spokespersons to whom officialdom is urged to listen, can be grouped into at least three classes: The angry egotistic megaphones; the rational educated diplomats; and the disenchanted traditionalists wanting to return to an earlier Utopia but who are devoid of constructive suggestions for their grandchildren's well-being.

Each state appears to have its Alpha 'Angrybird', its loud impatient uncompromising campaigner, always on their high horse, always dominating the microphone and always switching -off potential mainstream empathisers. Their personalities are always that of the self-serving publicist, the self-promoting egotist, the unabashed narcissist who feeds off public attention and media exposure. The informed rationalists in the mob are embarrassed by these puerile performers and recognise that this behaviour harms their cause. Nobody of influence listens, in fact they go on the defensive, put up their shutters and repeat their official mantra that without adult discussion we're unlikely to achieve a meeting of the minds. The message to these spruikers is: If you seek more listening, you must demonstrate competence in mature respectful debate. As Gary Johns remarked: 'What this lot needs is not more rights, but more good behavior.'

The second group, the rational diplomats, do get listened to. They receive a polite hearing and at least indications of serious consideration of their ideas. The third group, mostly elderly homelanders, gain empathy simply through their moral appeal to human decency and often evoke sentiments of support and sympathy, even if these are not followed up by practical plans to restore their comfort zone.

As for the inference that Aborigines are being ignored, there is much evidence to support such a claim. The more important question is not whether, but why, Aborigines perceive themselves to be ignored. This perception stems from the poverty and dysfunction they see in their communities. However the statistics on government spending per capita tells a very different story. This leads to the 'efficiency' debate which is based on how effective the spendings are, notably in remote communities. The short answer is they're not being ignored, but the inappropriate way in which they make their demands does their case harm. So when their firebrands not only lose goodwill but publicly bag their own more enlightened leaders, they cause double jeopardy for their people's case.

As for Pearson's longheld view on 'too much (recent) positive discrimination with adverse results, driven by White guilt, and perpetuating Indigenous Australian victimhood', he is spot-on and gets no argument from me. Though it must be said that contemporary mainstream youth and the 30% of Australians who are migrants, have justifiably distanced themselves from historic guilt. Back in 2007, Pearson wrote in the Griffith Review (Vol. 16) about White guilt, saying: 'Australia must be done once and for all with feelings of guilt and national shame over past discriminatory policies and current inadequate outcomes.' He asked for an end to Australia's history of Indigenous policy failure and a guarantee of equal rights and responsibilities for his people, like all other citizens. How welcome it would be if the large number of loud martyrists would heed Pearson's heartfelt appeal – an appeal which defines the stature of the man, a giant among pygmies.

Six

'More than half the Indigenous population receives most of their income from government welfare.'

This quote is based on the Review of Government Service Provision (2007) and brings the socio-economic situation into stark relief. Analysts will want to know what the comparative proportion of non-Indigenous citizens is, who depend majorly on welfare. As the population ages, this proportion will increase, but moving the majority of Aborigines who are on 'handouts', to practical 'handups' is a widely-held aspiration. The present situation was countered by the Abbott government's mantra: 'Kids in school, adults at work and families in their safe homes.' There is little opposition to this motherhood statement, but achieving this will take a long time.

Policy formulation obviously needs to focus on why the present level of government dependency is so high. Is it oppressive policy or is it irresponsible citizens which cause this dependency? Both is the answer and Pearson knows it.

Seven

'There is also a significant risk that Indigenous Australians will become as culturally impoverished as they are socio-economically… As Western market forces bear down on traditional Indigenous ways of life, cultural isolation is often the result. Only 18 of the previous 250 languages, are still spoken by all generations within a community… 100 languages still exist but 90 are near extinction. The 2009 Social Justice Report predicts that "without intervention, the language knowledge will cease to exist in the next 10 to 30 years". There is little government action to slow this steady decline.'

The extent and process of linguistic decline is now recognised and understood, but 'cultural impoverishment' of Aborigines is not exactly a priority concern for mainstreamers who are often battling to stay afloat financially as 'the end of entitlement' (as the Teasurer called it) comes to an end. The reason for this apathy is probably that the majority don't recognise any particularly valuable aspects of what they see as an outdated primitive culture, unaware of the ancient and sophisticated social mores of the Indigenous family and land relations.

The majority probably also regard 'cultural assimilation' as a plus for Aborigines, rather than a threat. The contrasting views of assimilation, as either a positive or negative process, is at the heart of the Recognition debate. History tells us that only the cultural speakers of a language become committed to saving their mother-tongue. My advice would be, don't wait for government, do it yourselves, when it comes to cultural rescue – and don't be surprised if your coming generations don't share your passion. That's just the way it has always been. Ask the other global Indigenous peoples.

Eight

'Consultation with Indigenous people has indicated that Indigenous Australians feel excluded from the Australian nation. They feel that they do not belong. They feel as though white Australians hate them. These findings should be a cause of great sadness for the nation. The challenge is to move from exclusion to inclusion.'

Everyone who overstates their (different) identity probably feels somewhat excluded from a tolerant multicultural society. Do Jews feel excluded? Do Muslims feel excluded? Do Afrikaners feel excluded? The difference is that Aborigines have consciously let the mainstream pass them by. Of course they don't belong if they're not doing what everyone else is doing, i.e. learning and earning. This is tough when you come from a culture which had no work ethic.

So if we are unsure about what 'un-Australian behaviour' means, then we should try 'un-Indigenous'. There is an original or traditional Aboriginality and a modern Aboriginality. The former focuses on customary norms, the latter on adopted partial-ly-assimilated norms. Is the former identity more authentic? When measured by productive adoptees, no. If you feel excluded, look inward, don't search for why the expected welcoming society is so reluctant to embrace you until you've nutted out why the birds of a feather don't flock together with you. However, it's not always your fault alone, if you don't feel that you 'belong'.

Belonging is a two-way achievement to which both individual and group contribute. [I am a mature-age migrant who fled Apartheid. I came here because I judged Australian norms to approximate the universal humanitarian values which my family stood for. I was not influenced by the earlier the White Australia policy or the present condition of the Aborigines, both of which I regarded as par for the course in former British colonies. Nor was I put off by Australia's convict forefathers, but having lived a while in England, I welcomed the 'classless' society, as advertised by the local Australian embassy in Pretoria.]

Returning to Pearson's statement that some Aborigines, 'feel they are hated by whites', a few comments are warranted. Firstly, I suggest that blatant hatred is probably rather rare, since this emotion is a reflection of fear or a perceived threat. Whites surely have nothing to fear and are certainly not threatened by Aborigines as a group. Secondly, I believe that this hateful comment is largely unfounded and should probably not have been made – certainly not in a serious research document on constitutional recognition. Reverse hatred would be much more justifiable, given Aboriginal history.

These sentiments on genetically-based comparisons should be deleted from contemporary debate, since they only serve to remind us of a bygone era when Social Darwinism and Imperial fervour combined to give Europeans an exalted view of themselves. Nevertheless, it behoves us to empathise with both parties in the mismatch of first contact. Have we asked whether there are white indigenes in some countries, and if so, how they compared culturally and intellectually to their invaders? When my ancestral Picts, Celts and Anglos were invaded by the Vikings, did they change their culture, adapt to good ideas of the newcomers, or did they forever complain that they suffered cultural genocide? When the Saxons and Angels where invaded first by the Romans, then by the Normans, did they demand that their identity be respected, that their languages be maintained, that a Treaty was required? No, the Brits lost out because the invaders were stronger, more organised and more technologically advanced. This is the story of the world, it was ever thus, except when Moses entered Canaan with his Israelites. In that case, they invaded a *terra nullius* because the Lord had smitten the Hittites in their ancestral country, or so the Old Testament records.

So it is a moot point as to whether the Aborigines were 'inferior' to the newcomers. What is important is that there was a mismatch, a clash of cultures and a perception by the newcomers that these stone-age occupants could be recognised as a culture but not as a civilisation in the normal understanding of the concept. Perhaps the colonisers could be forgiven for judging the locals on their lack of buildings, roads, bridges, wheeled vehicles, glazed pottery, smelters, fabrics, domestic animals and planted crops. While these deficiencies didn't make them sub-human, it may be fair to suggest that in the eyes of the newcomers, it made them pre-civilised. As such, it was unreasonable to treat them as equals when they clearly weren't, at least not by late 1700 European criteria. This did not mean that the locals lacked potential, but the retrospective expectations that they should have been given full Civil rights, even pre-Darwin, is to misunderstand human nature and racial competitiveness.

Despite this mismatch of two groups, the British Colonial office sought to protect the Aborigines' rights to maintain their traditional hunter-gatherer rights; rights which were usurped by settlers and by some colonial governors who consciously turned a blind eye to what was genteelly referred to as 'dispersal' of uncooperative Blacks.

Nine

*'None of these [policy] approaches have achieved the correct balance
– a balance which respects unique Indigenous culture and identity,
while allowing for full and equal participation in opportunities
and benefits of Australia's Western liberal economy... The colonised,
assimilated person lives a lie and is oppressed in Australia.*

*[He is] an Indigenous person who must suppress his culture in order
to realise socio-economic prosperity, he is not free... True freedom
means freedom to be yourself. The rights-driven era [of the 60s and
70s] saw a new respect for cultural difference... But the land rights
era post-Mabo, arguably swung too far in the opposite direction – the
direction of cultural relativism (all equally valuable) and collectivism
(communalism) at the expense of individual rights and individual
equality, driven by a misguided interpretation of 'self-determination', as mere separatism and collective treatment of indigenous
Australians.'*

This statement contains several concepts vital to Aboriginal futures.
The first is the concept of balance between personal identity and
modern well-being. There is probably a long continuum of views
on the most desirable level of cultural definition for transitioning individuals. The more culture-conscious Aboriginal leaders
continue to insist that Aborigines faced with overbearing Western
lifestyles, become culturally bereft and as a result, they become
'lost' and, it is said, may even 'lose their souls'. The question
then arises as to whether the well-being of the children is actually
reduced by the values of 'culturally appropriate' parents.

Pearson's 'full and equal participation' in the mainstream, will
inevitably dilute cultural identity. As a result, the 'freedom to be

179

yourself' brings important responsibilities for the self-identifying individual. The hard truth is that we are all bound to limit 'being ourselves' to behaviours which are accepted and expected by both our contemporary law and our majority's moral code. It is precisely these standards which characterise civil society and distinguish it from barbarism. Curbing of natural instincts is integral to social progress. Personal identity, values and behaviours which don't affect others, notably co-workers and neighbours, are socially unimportant, but 'being yourself' in a noisy, inconsiderate, rude and untidy way, soon highlights an individual's unsuitability for normal suburban life and work. This constraint applies equally to the Bogans of the Western Suburbs and to the Long-Grassers of Darwin.

This constraint also leads to a realisation that Pearson's concept of 'misguided interpretation of self-determination' is more than 'mere separatism and collective treatment' of Indigenous people and is of central significance. It is obvious that many Aborigines live a conflicted life which sits somewhat uncomfortably with Pearson's claim that: 'We contend that cultural recognition and equality are wholly compatible...just as rights are tied to responsibilities.'

Self-determination is potentially a long sequence of steps in increasing autonomy from local government to independent states then to sovereign nation, and finally to separate ceded entity. Pearson's reference to 'misguided interpretation' of self-government is a warning against losing coherent national unity in an Australia which must avoid separation if all its citizens are to benefit from tolerant diversity. This inclusive architecture is at odds with many aggressive Aboriginal separatists, whose fervour for an independent, sovereign Aboriginal nation, apparently also embraces the negative features which such notional apartheid will foist upon their coming generations.

Ten

'[Historically] assimilation and protectionism [were used] to implement integration at the expense of Indigenous culture, identity, families and Indigenous equal rights. The self-government era was effective in securing separate identities and lands, but ineffective in addressing poverty, in respecting individual rights, in allowing economic participation and in maintaining social norms, law and order, and communalism safely... While welfare reform has been successful [in some aspects] it has arguably not done enough to prevent cultural loss and extinction of Indigenous languages. Until equality before the law is an over-riding presumption, Indigenous Australians will still not truly be given a fair go. We contend that cultural recognition and equality are wholly compatible.'

The pros and cons of assimilation have already been referred to above, but the somewhat different idea of 'integration' needs to be distinguished, since both terms have become dirty words to the cultural purists. Without attempting a definitional difference between these terms, be assured that both are seen by some as leading to 'cultural genocide' and loss of identity. As such, both of these are seen as threats, despite the fact that many progressive Aborigines regard both these concepts, not only as new opportunities, but as indispensable platforms for the success of future generations.

So we return to the earlier question of the extent to which we as individuals allow ourselves to be defined by cultural identity. If cultural recognition and equality are 'wholly compatible' as Pearson contends, there should be no problem with assimilating or integrating, but in practice, the culturists seem to have lingering doubts as to whether they're selling out to the Whitefella, reneging on their customary duties and failing to keep the faith with their ancestors, whose spirits just won't go away.

This brings us to the general view that as science and technology progress, so spirituality and belief systems diminish, as guiding forces in modern life. In this way, the believers become viewed as old-fashioned, stuck in a religious timewarp in which 'primitive' beliefs are regarded as out-dated and unhelpful in modern living. How else might we explain our estimated 13% church-going population?

Finally, it should be emphasised that this comment is only on selected extracts of the Pearson/Morris submission. The Constitutional elements of the submission have been dealt with elsewhere.

PEARSON'S
END THE GUILT

The bloody colonial history of Australia has been recorded by many writers. Henry Reynolds produced a series of books sympathetic to the plight of the Aborigines, including his grandmother. Geoffrey Blainey gave us the choice of two opposing historical narratives: the Three Cheers version or the Black Armband version. More recently, Timothy Bottoms has produced a detailed catalogue of all recorded massacres.

Over the decades, Australia has developed what Deputy PM Tim Fisher called 'The Guilt Industry', driven largely by Aboriginal activists but spurred on by a range of commentators sympathetic to those who had lost their land, their culture, their language and finally, their children – the Stolen Generation. Local history is almost devoid of cases where sympathetic Whites sided with the Aborigines and supported their cause. But there are cases of individuals who went against the trend, such as those noble souls in Pamela Lukin Watson's book 'Frontier Lands And Pioneer Legends'.

There are others as well, who spoke out against the inhumane treatment meted out to Aborigines, not only in the early days of the Native Police under White officers, but also in more recent times – right up to 1967 when full citizenship was granted to Aborigines by a 91% 'Yes' vote in the national referendum.

Aboriginal activists have seldom missed the opportunity to

blame White policy for Black oppression, leaving present Whites ambivalent about the actual level of guilt by association. In a population founded on Christian tradition, the Golden Rule of 'Doing unto Others' has been hard to demonstrate in past Black/White relations. At the same time, today's young people justifiably wash their hands of previous generations' sins and feel little personal guilt about historic conflict. Migrants from non-Anglo countries also feel no responsibility for 'sins of the fathers', even if they are well aware of the less than humanitarian treatment of minorities in their own country.

Many contemporary politicians and their voters, would like all this guilt baggage to just go away, to be put forever into the past to concentrate on creating a better future for everyone. At the same time, there is a widely-held view that policy on Aboriginal welfare has reflected an unspoken guilt complex. It is this mindset which Noel Pearson first referred to as 'Passive Welfare', meaning that labour-free income had caused a damaging assumption of entitlement, which demotivated all recipients of the dole, and as a result acted as a disincentive for individuals to contribute to the real economy. For the past decade, Pearson's criticism of both policy and his own people's acceptance of low social expectations has led governments of various persuasions to seek ways of extracting the nation from what were guilt-laden welfare policies – despite the seldom acknowledgement of the guilt element. Pre-Keating (in June 2005), Noel Pearson made a public statement to the effect that whites must drop their guilt and look ahead to achieving equality for all.

What Pearson probably sought was to reach a position where:

i.   The mainstream and the politicians dropped feelings of

historic responsibility for the present Aboriginal situation and concentrated on rational socio-economic logic in encouraging individual responsibility.

ii. The Aborigines and their leaders ended the blame game, and recognised that some reasons for the present dysfunction lie with the people themselves, not necessarily with imposed policy or repressive regulations.

Several questions need to be asked about this important guilt statement which came from an Aboriginal, albeit out of left field: Why has this 'drop the guilt' concept been so long in coming from the Aboriginal camp? Is Pearson the first to state the sentiment so clearly, or is it just that it has come from this unusual visionary? The answers to these questions will affect the way in which activists find the wind being taken out of their sails.

This 'guilt question' leads on logically to the 'thanks question' which is the acknowledgement of what the intrusion of Western values and lifestyle have given the Aborigines. Once we can get over the fog of complaints about how the locals were treated by the newcomers, we should be able to compare the daily life of the old people in 1788 with the comforts and conveniences on offer, but not always taken, today.

In 'Jean's Story' (Roberts, 2017), the Aboriginal university student from Cape York suggests that together with NAIDOC week, the Aborigines should consider a Thanksgiving day. This would not be the same as the American Thanksgiving which thanks God for all their blessings. Jean's national day answers the question: where would we be without the newcomers? Jean pedals this idea around her campus mentors, virtually all of whom don't think it would gain her fellow Aboriginal Australian's approval. Why?

Because it puts an end to guilt and moral debt of the majority, and an end to martyrism and compensation claims of this minority. But Jean's not having it. She has convinced herself that having mastered only hunting, gathering and reproducing in 50,000 years at least, it was most unlikely that without an external trigger, her mob would have advanced far from the cave. She ponders whether the Dutch, Portuguese, Chinese or Indonesians would've done a more benign enlightenment job on her civilisation laggards. Would they have had to wait for some other visitors to show them a wheel, a glazed pot, a copper smelter, a stonemason's gear, a weaving loom, a steam engine or an artist's easel and oils? Or would they have eventually figured these out themselves or possibly visited an Asian neighbour, taking note of their technology?

Many peoples have adapted positively to the arrival of dominant newcomers. These Indigenous peoples were only pacified with the signing of a Treaty if they were regarded as a military threat, as with the Zulus in South Africa and the Maori in New Zealand. Why would the newcomers otherwise seek formal agreement to settlement of their lands? Clearly the relationship between first and second peoples changed since Moses invaded Canaan after the Lord had smote the Hittites, or since Genghis Khan, Atilla the Hun and the Vikings, used the 'might is right' principle to change the map of national boundaries. The British had the misfortune to still be colonising late in the global development of human rights, even after the abolition of slavery. It was for this reason that the Home Office had given James Cook, and then colonial governors, strict instructions not to disturb the natives and to ensure that settlement didn't usurp their right to occupy and hunt on their tribal lands.

Clearly a number of later governors were pressured by the local squattocracy, who dominated the early state parliaments, to turn a blind eye to the travesties occurring on the frontiers, where settlers became a law unto themselves. The latter-day demonstrators who blame the British government for ignoring their own Magna Carta, need to do their homework on the actual causes of conflict after first contact.

Returning to Pearson's 'end the guilt' appeal, the present consideration of constitutional change to recognise Australia's First People could benefit from this all-important aspect of the whiteman's psyche. This is not the place to analyse the merits of the various proposals on constitutional change, except perhaps to add to the mix, two more questions: Whose Constitution is this, and if change is in order, should God now be dropped from our founding documents? If the argument for change is based on the fact that this document was worded in an era when racial prejudice was much more overt, perhaps the same time-lapse applies to changes in religious belief.

For decades, the treaty-seekers have compared our situation with the Treaty of Waitangi in New Zealand. The matter gained new life in 1988 when PM Bob Hawke personally committed to signing a Treaty at the emotive Barunga Festival in the Territory, where he was presented with a formal log of claims from the Aborigines of that region. Today the relation of the Constitution to a Treaty probably warrants more air-time than it's had in the contemporary debate on recognition. The latest focus of this debate has been between symbolic and real constitutional changes. In other words, are we serious about improving the lot of Australian Aborigines?

PEARSON'S BLUEPRINT FOR EMPOWERED COMMUNITIES

Noel Pearson's blueprint for Aboriginal development is titled 'Empowered Communities: Empowered Peoples: Design Report'. It was released on 27/03/15 and given extensive coverage by 'The Weekend Australian', headlined 'Pearson's Beacon of Hope'. Because the report combines the input of Aboriginal leaders from eight communities, including two urban, it is offered as a national design report only.

The eight leaders were clearly not chosen at random, but rather according to the location of known progressive groups. Informed observers would have no trouble suggesting eight alternative communities devoid of enlightened leaders and councils, but this report was not meant to be representative.

This non-random selection of communities should not detract from the strength and logic of the substance of the Empowered Report, of which the cornerstone is the 'opt-in' clause. This alone distinguishes this blueprint from previous policies. Critics will immediately ask about those communities which decide to 'opt-out'. The answer is that they will miss out on the funding of projects which keep children in school, adults in work and well-housed communities in safety. The carrots and sticks offered, appear to be well-balanced and reflect the essential principle of individual responsibility Pearson has championed for nearly two decades.

There is probably general agreement with one participating leader who reported that these are not new ideas, in fact they are well-known proposals whose time had finally come. In the past, Pearson has always been careful to stress that he speaks only for his Cape York people. He's long been aware of how strongly each People feel about speaking for themselves. However, when the Federal Government apparently passed him over, in favour of Warren Mundine, as chair of the Indigenous Advisory Council, PM Abbott invited him to lead a new body on Sustainable Communities. Whether Pearson actually turned down the advisory chairmanship is not known, but his present challenge has, at last, given him the Federal imprimatur to lift his vision beyond Cape York and recommend national-scale guidelines – something which PM Howard did informally back in 2000 after Pearson offered his policy guidelines.

While the reference to key concepts may be different in the full report, the absence of some basic concepts from the columns of several commentators, is more than a little surprising. Most students of Aboriginal policy will be well aware of the stark divide within the Aboriginal community between the traditionalists and modernists. While there is a considerable rump of nuanced middle-ground, the former group, place great stock in culture and clan identity. They play down the need for a work ethic and thus for skills education. 'Culturally appropriate' is their catch-cry. They interpret every move toward the mainstream's lifestyle as a further step toward cultural genocide. Loss of clan identity, loss of respect for tradition, and loss of language, all reinforce the central loss of country as unforgivable acts of oppression which forever martyrise the survivors.

The modernists or 'joiners' on the other hand, while not

wanting to lose their First People identity, accept the reality of employment and thus the basic need for schooling and income-generating skills. It is this enlightened group to whom Pearson has always appealed. Once again he's pushing individuals' 'right to take personal responsibility'. Once again he's inviting his people to grasp the opportunity to break out of their stultifying remote poverty cycle. To distance themselves from their norm-free ghetto lifestyle.

Paul Kelly, Editor-at-Large for 'The Australian', uses the subtitle 'Noel Pearson is redesigning the Indigenous contract' in his 'Radical Blueprint' column. Many will argue that Kelly misses the important point that there is in fact no Indigenous contract. What there currently is, is a one-sided, imposed program which is largely planned and implemented by mainstream government with insufficient consultation with those at the receiving end.

Interestingly, Pearson refers to the Empowered Report as 'the culmination of my work over the past 15 years. If I have any contribution to make to public policy in Australia, this is it.' Pearson clearly sees his group's blueprint as more than guidelines for the eight regions represented. In fact, he claims, 'we really need to be a beacon for the rest of Indigenous Australia.' Using well-known Pearsonesque language, he explains the contemporary Indigenous position as follows: 'We are left as mendicants within the majoritarian system of democracy. We cannot effectively influence decisions which most affect our lives.'

This sentiment may well be justified, but the question of the cause of this situation looms large as a sequitur. A hardy perennial element of the 'Aboriginal problem' has been the blame-shifting between people and policy, i.e. are we in this predicament because we are a mob of slackers, or because good, but damaged, people are prevented by policy, from lifting themselves out of dysfunction? This is not the place to once again argue the toss on responsibility, but clearly the Empowerment Report challenges communities to meet its 'three tiers or tests: development, empowerment and productivity'. This Holy Trinity is aimed at 'changing the current mindset'. By re-badging government from 'rescuers' to 'enablers' the whole game changes – or does it?

We presume that to become empowered the individual and community require, as a basic ingredient, the desire to change. This desire, in turn, is predicated on a sufficient level of dissatisfaction with the *status quo*, to motivate individuals to act. Paul Kelly asks the central question: 'Is the Indigenous community leadership up to the job?' Kelly is reflecting the doubts of many experienced policy-watchers, about the long-recognised leadership vacuum. The old 'flying with eagles when working with turkeys' idiom looms large. Firstly, the turkeys may not be responsible for being turkeys. Secondly, flying like an eagle is not the turkey's forte, so if eagles want them to soar to new heights, they may have to accept that a long transition period of turkey-to-eagle may require the patience of Job and a considerably less aloof or egocentric leadership style by some of the eagles.

Pearson envisages 'a new centre of gravity' in Indigenous affairs. However this novel fulcrum may not be inherently beneficial, because if the gravity does not originate from the majority of community individuals, the leader will be charging ahead on his own. This means that Kelly's questioning of leadership's capacity should rather be aimed at the followers. If the mob have no initiative, we can expect leaders of the 'Yes Minister' type – as Jim Hackett said: 'I am their leader, I must follow them.'

There has long been the possibility of dissatisfied clan members leaving their dysfunctional remoteness, but their personal capacity to grab this opportunity has repeatedly been overstated by politicians. South Australian studies show clearly what traits characterised the 'movers'. As a corollary, these studies highlighted the shortcomings of the 'stayers' who, not necessarily because of inherent inability, had become immobile. Pearson's blueprint offers both on- and off- country wealth-generating challenges, but the large proportion of generationally-unemployed males in the Native Title lands will remain a brake on the uplifting of many remote communities. The urban communities are very different in that they out-marry at a rate of over 80% and largely compete in the mainstream economy, through better education.

Anyone who has studied Pearson's 'Up from the Mission' (2009) will recognise the origin of the building blocks of the Empowered Report. In that collection of papers, Pearson gives credit to several thinkers from whom he gleaned new insights, including the Right to take Responsibility. The term 'radical' has lost its original meaning of getting to the root of an issue and has come to mean 'different from the present, usual, common or generally understood position' on an issue'. The radical element of the Empowered blueprint is its 'opt-in' basis – a sort of self-selected commitment in which financial and social benefits are gained by volunteering groups. Such incentives are precisely what has been missing from previous do-gooder schemes which had no incentive to change, and indeed, discouraged personal initiative.

Pearson's word choice in describing the current funding model as 'sclerotic' is unhelpful, although it has been used by other writers. Sclerosis is an abnormal hardening of body tissues. Several other medical analogies related to diet and exercise would be more apt. On the other hand, Pearson's comparison with the 30-year-old

National Competition Policy is apt in the way he compares Australia's earlier protectionist and highly-regulated trade policy, with Indigenous funding.

This blueprint will probably succeed if it delivers a strategy by which empowerment can be achieved in practice. 'Blueprint' is a term which refers to a visible plan of how all segments of construction fit together, but it omits the 'how to' details. This is conceded when the report declares: 'delivery is the key to success.' This is more than the bleeding obvious, it is the only test of the real worth of this report.

So what's new, observers will ask.

i.   The program is 'opt-in', unlike previous programs.

ii.   It invites individuals to give initiative and be responsible.

iii. It values productivity and financial independence.

iv.   It doesn't dwell on culture or tradition, but recognises their value without allowing them to define the participants.

v.   It focuses on future generations' needs rather than the values of current seniors.

vi.   It includes an Indigenous Policy Productivity Council to monitor the effectiveness of implementation. This body will check how the bottom-up model works, but its members should never forget why the top-down approach was decided on in earlier years.

Parliamentary Secretary to the Prime Minister, Alan Tudge, in an effort to demonstrate the disjointed nature of present services, used the Roebourne (WA) example. In this community of 1150, he found 67 provider agencies implementing 400 programs funded by Federal and State governments – that's one program for every three people. In housing, the Territory charged nearly $10 million to administer house construction valued at $2.7 million. In 2012-13, the states spent $30 billion on Aboriginal and Islander services, of which $5.6 billion was 'Indigenous Specific'. So Australia currently spends $21,000 on each of its non-Indigenous citizens and $43,500 on each Indigenous individual, as claimed by Tudge in the Empowered Report.

Because the bulk of spending is on social services and welfare, this situation should change significantly if Empowerment succeeds. The proof will lie in the number of communities which opt-in and succeed over the next five years or so. This in turn will depend on how much 'skin in the game' communities have, to use a well-worn Pearsonism.

Critics at Hall's Creek are already asking why individuals who have shown no responsibility to date, should be given the choice of opting-in. Thus the concept of 'deserving' has already been raised. This is the other side of the argument which holds that individual freedom is being strangled by passive welfare.

I've visited Hall's Creek, Fitzroy Crossing and Alice Town camps and come away with an overwhelming feeling that without replacing separate development with integration, there seems little hope of raising the norms and thus the advancement of such communities. Surely there are ways of articulating the benefits of integration and ending its 'dirty word' connotation. Shifting government from rescuers to enablers may require very different human raw materials than those presently available in many remote communities.

It is noteworthy that none of the early commentators on this report mention the absence of self-government, independence, freedom or sovereignty, as serious concepts in the blueprint, concepts so dear to the People's Congress and the Freedom Summit. What does this say about acceptance of Pearson's governance model by the mob?

Any serious critique of the substance of the Empowered Report must include a somewhat broader vision than Pearson's, of the possible shifting geographic location of future communities. At the risk of accusations of paternalistic social engineering, any visionary must offer serious changes to the location of many of the present (and currently non-existent) Aboriginal 'communities' as generally understood. Not only should the Torres Strait Islanders be treated as the different and separate people that they are, but it should be openly agreed that many of the present community locations are:

i.   Not the actual clan country of the present people.
ii. Are incapable of developing a human carrying capacity of viable size, largely because of insufficient water.
iii. Are currently devoid of the required human capital to give sufficient momentum to real empowerment.
iv. Are unlikely to respond to a range of incentives or disincentives.
v.   Fall so far short of meeting what is expected of a real productive community. This means that attempts to empower them may be flogging a dead horse. Pearson knows this and is going with the goers as a first step toward broader empowerment.

This negative assessment in no way diminishes Pearson's possibility of gaining a goodly number of viable takers for his plan, but it does beg the question of whether a dichotomy of empowered and other communities cries out for a clear plan of action for the opt-outers. We await Blueprint #2, remembering this is only the Design Report.

For two decades, 'The Australian' has fudged the reality that Pearson in fact may not have the backing of most people in Cape York, as we saw in the Wild Rivers saga. The truth is that Pearson's noble rhetoric and striking articulation have always been way ahead of most of the mob, including many of his own mob. As a result, the implementation of the Empowerment plan will need a considerable period of bringing the remote dwellers up to speed on required expectations and personal responsibility requirements, before real economies replace the artificial economy they've been brought up on.

Whatever proposals from the Empowered Report are accepted for implementation, let us hope that when Pearson said 'This is it', referring to the culmination of his life's work, he wasn't announcing his retirement from the field. Whether they are considered radical or contentious, the gravity of Pearson's ideas have outweighed all others in this policy arena – as Peter Beattie reminded us. Thus, while most of us are aware of Pearson's recent health challenges, it is hard to imagine Indigenous policy formation without his dominating input.

Empowered Communities (EC):
The Recommendations
Noel Pearson's Empowered Report makes many sensible proposals in its ten pages of recommendations. In essence, it requests government to agree, affirm, recognise and adopt several dozen goals, agreements and policies which advantage Indigenous

communities who have opted-in to the proposed policy framework. In all, it is a healthy mix of incentives, responsibilities, rights and benefits, which flow from community initiative aimed at self-determined equal citizenship.

At its base level, the policy seems to represent rules of engagement for what some might see as Black Local Government by another name, but fundamentally they're racial local governments with benefits. Clearly a report as wide-ranging as this, invites experienced policy-observers to ask many questions about the basic assumptions of this comprehensive policy proposal. This is only the Design Report but some questions remain:

6. Will this report encourage or discourage those who have the choice, to opt for Indigenous status as individuals? Who defines Indigenous status and should we be keeping current criteria?

7. Is it not better to define empowered groups by geography rather than race or First People?

8. If local government is driven by income from rates, should income streams be considered more seriously in the report?

9. With the continuing strong call for autonomy, sovereignty, freedom and independence by Indigenous spokespersons, why does the report settle for self-determination while ignoring sovereignty as a goal?

10. What happens to funding in those communities who don't opt-in? Are the criteria for allowing further communities to opt-in, clear enough?

11. With over 80% of Indigenous people already urbanised, isn't disproportionate attention given to empowering

remote communities and their traditional values?

12. By using the racial criterion of 'Indigenous' as the golden thread of eligibility for inclusion, the opportunity to address *poverty* and *need* as the central problem, is overlooked. Isn't this serious?

13. The importance of personal country to homelands inhabitants is appreciated, but the reason for emphasis on a 'place-based' development agenda seems out of place when all developments actually refer to a particular location. Should not the idea of 'place-based' agendas be qualified as non-urban?

14. Are not all population groups free to preserve, maintain and adapt their cultural heritage? If so, the concept of 'deserving' falls away.

15. Cultural recognition and respect cannot be legislated. Should the report not emphasise that respect from other groups must be earned and demonstrated through achievement? Being first is insufficient.

16. While decision-making at the closest level to those affected is reasonable, surely a veto is necessary on developments that have serious environmental impacts. Doesn't the demand for local priorities seriously impinge on financial responsibilities of ratepayers?

17. Are empowered communities based on real economies or on a socially disguised cost-shifting mechanism which allows only one racial group to receive benefits in excess of both their economic input and output?

18. Many urban regions have non-Indigenous householders interspersed with Indigenous members. Doesn't it make sense to drop the racial qualification for geographical

groupings? Who defines the boundaries?

19. Is not the concept of 're-establishing Indigenous authority' a legal minefield of inevitable insoluble conflict?

20. The phrase 'rights of all community members are recognised and respected under the law…and under cultural values', lacks clarity on whether 'traditional law' operates or not. Should not the envisaged role of Indigenous Law (and medicine) be made clear, as integral elements of empowerment?

21. With all the emphasis on identity and culture in the report, why are local decisions on exclusively Indigenous foster parents avoided?

22. 'First priorities for reform are firstly advocated by leaders of Empowered Communities (EC's) and secondly supported by governments. It is at its core, about aboriginal culture, not government policy.' Doesn't this paragraph (15) lead to the question of whether it is best for the grandchildren, if adults insist on being defined by an ancient culture which offers little for modern living.

23. Does the report support the Elder system of governance, and if so, is this only in remote homelands, or are city dwellers supported in their adopted democracy?

24. 'There is a reciprocal obligation on governments and others within the wider Australian community to ensure that Indigenous people are welcomed and their children and young people are treated with respect and dignity…' This statement is referring to First Peoples in the EC pursuing their First Priorities, but the concept of an obligated mainstream avoids the idea of deserving or warranting respect. As Gary Johns suggested, what's required is not

more rights but more good behaviour. If the report is trying to say discrimination must stop, should it not just say so?

25. The recommendations on governance (21-24) would have gained more support if a clear urban/rural dichotomy was used as a framework for the report. The only thing these differentiated mobs have in common is a greater or lesser inheritance of Indigenous DNA. This highly variable common thread is an ineffective basis for serious policy-making for such a diverse group.

26. 'Governance arrangements will vary from region to region, including the terms of the arrangements put in place to ensure cultural authority is respected and appropriately engaged' (22). If this means the city mob may have moved on from this cultural authority, why doesn't it say so?

27. The only service outsourcing which is recommended is accounting services (28b). Why?

28. The recommendations stated that it is not clear whether current funding is sufficient to achieve what is required in Indigenous affairs. It is clear that current results don't match expenditure (30). The use of the concept of an Efficiency Dividend (31c) is long overdue, but what needs to be asked is why Indigenous leaders didn't push for this idea, by whatever name, decades ago.

29. The Right to Development (39) needs very serious quali-fication if inappropriate and unviable developments are to be prevented. The record is littered with disastrous failures of insufficient market research and management failure in Aboriginal affairs.

Overall, the report contains a range of sound design and planning ideas, many of which will take considerable time to implement. The report correctly expects adjustments and changes to be necessary as communities with different needs and abilities opt-in. If the ultimate goal is to achieve greatest benefit for the largest number of EC members, it follows that the best measure of investment efficiency will be the eventual number of communities invited into the EC members' list. Politically, success could be guaranteed by simply limiting entry to the EC to those few exemplary communities who meet all the entry criteria. If opting-in allowed unready groups to be welcomed into the EC group, the success rate after, say, five or ten years would probably be very low. The likely reason might be lack of appropriate leadership, motivation, education and skills, i.e. insufficient human capital.

The difference between empowered and viable, may be critical to an EC's future well-being. Alsop et al's (2005) idea of empowerment for UN assisted communities through the World Bank, has been used by many developing countries but branded by several names. An individual becomes empowered by education and skills, by the laws which allow one to compete fairly for jobs and housing, and by local government processes which take one's voice seriously. Viability by contrast, is the result of income-generation sufficient to make well-being attainable, given the necessary initiative and co-operation from individuals, to produce an economically viable community who value civil norms enough to ensure a socially functioning group of families.

It is a relief to taxpayers to read that the reporter's vision is to enable their children to compete in the mainstream while maintaining their identity. However, claiming that failure to progress is ultimately due to disempowerment cannot go unqualified. Similarly, with claiming that disempowerment includes 'not being able to get government to work for us as citizens'.

The report's 3% mouse analogy to extreme minority status of the dispossessed people excluded from the original constitution, overlooks the success of other equally small minorities who were dispossessed elsewhere.

Discussion

There are so many good ideas in this empowerment report that it is likely to become a milestone in Indigenous development. However, its Achilles' heel may be its over-emphasis on separatism and its repeated assumption that different policy is required for Indigenous people. The report seems to assume that genetic origin is more important than need, in determining supportive policy for minorities whose original culture and religion were threatened. It may have carried more weight if the report had recognised the well-established urban communities as a diaspora of the original homeland communities, and had differentiated them on the basis of the need for opportunity and services. By insisting on the common thread of voluntary identification as First People, the report has once again fallen for the Coombsian thesis that cultural identity is the key to personal confidence and success.

Why mixed communities apparently cannot be led by non-Indigenous leaders is not clear. Why self-determination is more important for Indigenous Australians than other cultural groups is not proven. Why other groups should not be given equal empowerment opportunities, remains unanswered.

Insisting that current disempowerment is predominant-ly the result of discriminatory policy reflects a less than truthful acceptance of the reality of the limited capacity of an original People to adapt to progressive society norms. This view does not gainsay the trauma of colonial and post-colonial violence and discrimination, but rather reflects a more nuanced honesty as to the causes of the current situation.

Avoiding integration is stated as a goal of empowerment by one of the leaders in the report. It would have been useful if the report had used one of thousands of examples of successfully integrated Aborigines to demonstrate there are many kinds of empowerment, all of which can be achieved without loss of self-esteem and origin. The days of original tribal pride have long since receded in most developed societies and the appreciation of tolerant diversity is well-established in prosperous democracies which focus on unified national pride.

The report states up front that its goal is for Indigenous children to compete in the mainstream; a goal which all Australians would applaud. However, whether individuals should consider themselves as Australians first or Indigenous first, requires greater consideration than is given in this report.

The recommendations call for Aborigines to be recognised as 'equal citizens and recognised as the Indigenous peoples of Australia'. In this context 'equal' should not mean 'privileged' by the proposed policy. In this sense, the privilege is not so much financial as cultural, so the question arises as to who should pay for cultural preservation. History records how colonised countries, whether 'invaded' or not, invariably take on the values of the newcomers and how the preservation of the original culture almost always becomes the responsibility of that culture's members.

When the geographical boundaries of the empowered communities are determined, the so-called 'place-based' developments will have to be agreed to by a democratic process within the new 'local government' limits. I've repeatedly stressed the need for agreement on three fundamental but unasked, questions:

    i.   What is the most appropriate role for group identity and culture in multi-cultural Australia?

    ii.   What is the most effective form of local governance?

    iii. What level of self-determination (up to sovereignty) holds most promise for group well-being?

When the Empowered Report states that, 'The policy recognises the primacy of the local nature of people and places...' the implications of this for local planning requires explanation. And if the term 'subsidiarity' means 'bottom-up', it should say so for clarity's sake.

There has forever been tension between local, state and federal government, usually over the financial 'buck-passing' which occurs. In the case of Empowered Indigenous Communities, Pearson's proposals ask for a ten-year commitment to development agendas, 'not subject to chopping and changing with government changes'. Many local governments would say amen to that, especially in recent years when one-term state governments became more common.

In referring to First Priorities for reform, the report proposes policy which 'honours inherited cultures and traditions, including modern expressions of these values in response to contemporary life'. Such adaptation and inclusion of new cultural norms should be the total responsibility of the self-identified group. Whether others honour them, cannot be legislated.

It is assumed that the eight leaders who contributed to this report understand that no local development agenda can have its priority actions approved unless they meet the state and federal funding capacity for the region concerned. This means that no community in Australia can demand that its priorities be accepted and implemented simply because the locals agreed to these priorities. Environmental requirements, funding and economic viability, are all essential criteria for development approval. In addition, every Australian community's priorities must remain subject to planning and zoning requirements if dysfunctional development is to be avoided in the longer term. The idea that 'since you're an Indigenous community you can do as you like' is clearly taking empowerment beyond its reasonable meaning.

The intent of the demand-driven framework for purchases and contractors is clear and long overdue, but if it disregards market forces and ignores the basic laws of supply and demand and their effect on price, no local economy can be developed without significant waste of taxpayer money. Interpretation of the phrase: '[Ensuring] that regulatory approval processes are fair and take into account the development deficit in Indigenous communities', needs accurate information on the reasons for this deficit.

Finally, the statement that: 'there will only be one entry point to the Empowered Communities model in each region' will ring alarm bells among the democratically-minded citizenry. While the intention of the current leaders to control planning is clear enough in the single-point entry idea, the danger of monopolistic trends are real.

Overview

Opting-in means 'signing up to and abiding by EC reform policy'. Failure to carry out such agreement could lead to: 'action or review by the IPPC.' In addition, 'Poor governance or corrupt practice will prohibit an organisation from opting in.' In Cape York,

Pearson believes that EC funding arrangements should provide:

1. Greater long-term funding certainty, enabling opt-in EC's to pursue their strategic agenda.
2. Performance incentives.
3. An opt-in process which starts with the four C.Y. Welfare Reform communities.

Will the government accept the EC recommendations? Probably not *in toto*, although the potential for more effective spending should be very attractive to government. The creation of an 'opportunity support system', as envisaged in the McClure Report, should also be attractive to government since it is based on individual responsibility to gain skills for employment. The Empowered Report largely meets the current official mantra of 'kids in school, adults in work and families safe in their own homes.'

Pearson was right in pointing out (p 60) two major weaknesses in the recent (2014) Indigenous Advancement Strategy (IAS), notably:

1. Its lack of leadership reform.
2. The absence of a demand-driven system.

He was wrong in not crediting IAS with other worthy goals. Since the IAS process was aimed at precisely what Empowerment sought, i.e. more targeted and effective use of federal funds, it would have been useful had Pearson indicated the total cost and number of people who have actually gained from the unusually large Cape York investment to date. This would have allowed effectiveness to be compared with efficiency.

Pearson's recording of 'fighting among ourselves' (page 114) as a negative factor, is perhaps a more serious and widespread brake on progress than comes across in this report. This internal conflict and inability of families and clans to accept representation by others at a higher hierarchical level, has always bedeviled Aboriginal solidarity and their capacity to speak to government with a strong united voice. Pearson could have emphasised the need for a national voice, if that's what he believes is required. The failure of ATSIC, of the Congress of First Peoples, and currently of the Freedom Summit, offer telling examples of organisational failure which needs to be overcome if clear representative policy recommendations are to carry weight at federal level. However, the truth may be that because of the urban/remote nexus, there is in fact, no commonly-held Aboriginal view of the future. Pearson may thus be indicating by his opt-in mechanism that rather than seeking an inclusive unity for all, the new reforms should concentrate on the self-selected willing and able, and not let the laggards hold back the progressives, as in Keating's 'crabs in the bucket' analogy.

At the same time, a more pro-active community demand is required to stop the puerile inter-family conflict from preventing progress, than simply having Pearson make statements on the existence of these impediments. He is correct in claiming that local government and social control 'is often plagued by factional fighting, particularly along lines determined by family and cultural identification and membership'. He's also correct in stating that the influence of effective authority is too limited. The reason for this is perhaps not simply the imposed government control, but rather the lack of readiness of the community to take the democratic process seriously, as applied to regional and local government.

Pearson doesn't use this example, but his own Hopevale Council is a case in point. The questions Pearson asked of his own community when he fronted the local miscreants in 2009, still remain largely unanswered, notably those on their readiness to accept individual responsibility to uphold civil norms in Hopevale. The heartfelt prose of his seminal essay 'Hopevale Lost' has stirred even the dullest of minds. The hard truth is that Pearson was running too far ahead of the pack, and as a result, retreat by his detractors into the learned comfort zone of the welfare refuge continued to win the day. In such circumstances, the chances of being branded a divisive radical, rather than a redemptive saviour, were high. As a result, Pearson has decided that the movers and shakers should not be held back, waiting for the lowest common denominator to catch up. His alternative is to offer empowerment opportunities to those with enough insight to put their communal hands up.

This opt-in offer will be welcomed by many communities frustrated by what they see as a lack of prospects for their children. However, there will initially be many cases in which the present controlling families do not always reflect the progressive insights of significant proportions of the communities. These self-starters must initiate contact with the visiting Empowerment panels to commence progressive dialogue where narrow family-based inaction has prevented forward-looking empowerment in education, skills training and financial independence. In the same way, laggards within well-led opt-in communities will hopefully be swept along by the envisaged tide of economic emancipation.

Both of Pearson's structures for local co-ordination, i.e. Regional Steering Committees and Negotiation Tables, have considerable merit. Steering committee members will be elected or selected by the EC's to undertake nine functions of co-ordination and standards achievement across a geographical region. The Tables create a regional forum for negotiation with all levels of government in an effort to overcome past incoherence of funding. While the outcomes from Pearson's previous attempts to establish Negotiating Tables in Cape York could best be described as patchy, an invigorated and empowered branding of this idea may give more positive results. Hopefully the old resistance among some Cape York clans to anything that comes from Pearson will have dissipated this time around.

The final point to be made is that the contribution received from the Co-chair of this Empowerment group, namely Liza Carroll of the Prime Ministers Office, is difficult to find. This is disappointing and leaves readers wondering whether her role was purely as gatekeeper for government and whether as a result, she received a less than collegial reception from Pearson.

CONSTITUTIONS FOR DUMMIES[6]

Some years ago the Federal Goverment put up over $23 million for a Panel to recommend on Aboriginal recognition in Australian law. Many well informed commentators suggested their version of appropriate recognition and after the deadline for submissions closed, Paul Kelly of 'The Australian' claimed the whole process a fiasco.

Following the Panel, the Joint Parliamentary Committee on recognition, chaired by Ken Wyatt and deputised by Nova Peris, also reported. Paul Kelly describes that report as ambitious and idealistic, but deeply flawed. He doesn't mince his words: '[It] will only generate grief and dashed expectations…Assertions that it will lead to a successful referendum are a delusion.' He says Aboriginal leaders 'have fallen into a terrible trap', i.e. demanding non-discrimination in the Constitution, which Kelly guarantees will fail at a referendum.

Ever since constitutional change to recognise Australia's First People, the tussle between the symbolists and the substantialists has increased from a lackadaisical 'who cares?' to a demanding 'need for the Constitution to recognise us'.

---

[6] Since 2012 the process of constitutional Recognition of Indigenous peoples has been constantly changing, making it difficult for reviewers to offer contemporary opinion on this moving feast. Nevertheless the fundamental concepts in this debate remain significant whether encapsulated in the Constitution or Treaties.

The recognition game kicked off at the beginning of 2012 when the Labour government appointed the Expert Panel to look into the matter. The Panel recommended:

- Removing the race powers from the present constitution.
- Acknowledging Aborigines' relationship with the landscape.
- Permitting government to legislate for Aborigines as an identified group.
- Banning discrimination.

These changes were seen by some jurists as having problems of interpretation by the courts, and because constitutional changes require a referendum, the Panel's recommendations soon attracted the pragmatists who predicted a failure of such a poll. The wording of the referendum questions then became a central issue. Legal advice indicated that two sections of the Constitution were so outdated that they were no longer appropriate, i.e. Section 25 which disallowed certain races from voting, and section 51 (XXV1) which is the racial power section.

The combinations and permutations of legal, poetic, anti-racial, realistic, ideological and unashamedly political statements proposed for constitutional consideration, eventually sullied the waters of clear thinking. In the end, the confusion of strongly-held views were not nailed down to short, easily-understood statements and choices at the close of the submission period in June 2015.

Amongst the confusion, one thing became clear: if this matter is to go to a referendum, then absolute clarity on wording of options for voters is a necessity. With this in mind, the Prime Minister called a special meeting between forty Aboriginal leaders and himself, plus the opposition leader, to seek agreement on how the referendum wording should be determined. The main outcome of this meeting in Sydney was that a series of community meetings would be organised throughout the country in 2015-16 to seek consensus on referendum questions and their implications.

Having considered all the submissions for constitutional change, Greg Craven (The Australian 15/7/15) hit the nail on the head when he warned about giving the courts too much interpretive power. Craven agrees with my claim that unclear objectives are the basic cause of the present conflict of views: 'We now have a breather to consider exactly what we are trying to achieve and how.' This is precisely what the Expert Panel should have had as their terms of reference before they started their $23 million discussion.

It would not be surprising if virtually all those trained in Constitutional Law, as Craven is, agree with him when he says: 'So let's be blunt. None of the three options presented by the recent report of the Joint Parliamentary Committee will fly.' The central problem lies with the committee's attempt to illegalise government discrimination against only one minority group. Whether its proposal does represent what Craven calls a 'one-line bill of rights' is left in the hands of the judiciary and this he says could become a 'devil's playground'. The committee's other proposal is to insert into the Constitution broad statements acknowledging Indigenous people as first occupiers with special relationships to land and water, and (virtually) demanding respect for culture, language and heritage. Craven maintains that the issue is not whether we agree with such statements, but rather how the courts will interpret these statements. It is wrong to assume that these 'claims' are 'mere poetry' because in practice they could surpass Native Title as a Select Lawyer's Picnic without end. These statements will be seen by activists, and some judges, as a 'three paragraph bill of rights'.

These unrealistic demands are seen by some conspiracy theorists as a deliberately engineered attempt to ensure a knockback from mainstream Australia, demonstrating to the United Nations Indigenous Rights committee, that racial oppression remains alive and well in this world-leading multiculture. To solve the 'Aboriginal problem' (not a good phrase), Australia needs agreed decisions by all on:

i.   The benefits of unity over separation.

ii. The right of individuals to choose their own single, mixed or layered personal identity.

iii. The responsibility of each ethnic group to maintain their own culture.

iv. The extent to which the benefits of resource exploitation should be spread across the population.

v.   The role and effectiveness of homelands in enhancing well-being.

CONSTITUTION, EDUCATION AND VALUES

As the constitutional debate on Aboriginal recognition rolls relentlessly on, the matter of values, as reflected in our Constitution, begins to be subjected to more incisive scrutiny. Under the new spotlight is the way our founding document reflects the values which our nation holds dear. mongst these, apart from the rule of law, are the humanitarian norms which Australians believe to be worth stating, worth preserving and worth fighting for – and as Mandela said, worth dying for.

One faction of the commentariat hold that our recent emphasis on multiculturism and comparative cultures has led to an insidious devaluing of our majority Anglo culture. It is perhaps unsurprising that the conservatives, who were appointed by the Abbott government to supervise the development of an updated Australian national school curriculum, would respond to the growing cultural relativism by reminding us that our cultural heritage has been devalued by the unfounded push to declare all cultures of equal merit.

In these blurring circumstances, it was always predictable that a rearguard action would be mounted by the Anglo-Christian right, to rectify the unjust claims of minority cultures that the Christian colonisers had much to answer for, given the contemporary condition of the 'oppressed' in our society.

The Constitution is supposed to say who we are, by way of stating the things we stand for and how we treat others. It is thus fair enough to link the recent constitutional proposals to the values encapsulated in our education curricula. This allows us to link Greg Craven's constitutional philosophy with the educational philosophy of Kevin Donnelly. They're both from the Australian Catholic University, the former as Vice-Chancellor, the latter as co-chair of the governments Review of the National Curriculum. Both have no doubt been influenced by that earlier Catholic mentor Bob Santamaria, who was in turn, also one of Tony Abbott's early political mentors.

The matter at stake here is the comparative virtue of the Anglo-Christian sense of values which has taken a battering in recent years, notably from post-religious academics. The conservatives would like to see 'greater emphasis on Western civilisation' (Recommendation 15 of the curriculum review). Opposed to this is the unanimous view of another education organisation, the Australia Curriculum Studies Association. This body was set up to give a combined voice to subject associations, education academics and researchers who apparently all agree that 'it is wrong to privilege one civilisation over another' in Donnelly's words. (Weekend Australian 11/07/2015).

Recent barbaric terrorism in the Middle East, which has overflowed to suicide bombers terrorising several Western cities, has caused a re-think of what we stand for, leading the UK's leader David Cameron, to challenge his people to develop a stronger sense of their own identity, if they are to resist terrorism. This statement, (back in 2010), led to our Federal Government going to unusual lengths to upgrade border security, internal safety and international co-operation on security. Singing from the same hymn-sheet, Donnelly now calls for all Australians to 'advocate for our identity and way of life' in a way which positively re-assesses the virtues of our rule of law, our Westminster(-type) democracy, our separation of church and state and our (Christian) values including 'the sanctity of life'. These artefacts of our Western civilisation are seen as ensuring peace and prosperity, of guaranteeing legal and political rights, and the pursuit of happiness.

The defenders of our faith are saddened by the way the cultural relativists (all are good) shirk from defending the faith and remain silent when our values are publicly denigrated. Even Western civilisation is seen as having had its' day. The Curriculum Association's journal 'Curriculum Perspectives' has published several papers which insist that Judeo-Christianity is only one faith in the multi-faith Australian society, and as such, it should be considered alongside Islam, Buddhism, Agnosticism and Atheism.

The census of 2011 shows Christianity to still be the leading religion (61%), followed by No Religion (22%), Buddhism (2.5%), Islam (2.2%), Hinduism (1.3%) and Judaism (0.5%). There are no figures for Aboriginal religion or Animism. Kevin Donnelly quotes Tony Taylor of UTS as arguing that Judeo-Christianity is no more than a 'neo-conservative fabricated myth' which sounds to me much like Luther's original view on Catholicism. Taylor adds that even the unifying concept of Judeo-Christianity is insulting to both those religions. Other observers hold that multi-culturism itself is a tautology, a nonsense which ignores the way in which virtually all cultures have borrowed from others. Certainly the ideas of virgin birth, resurrection and the afterlife were borrowed from beliefs which predate Christ. In the same way, languages such as English, are unashamedly multi-lingual, drawing on a dozen other tongues.

So where does this leave our Constitution and contemporary attempts to acknowledge First People and their culture? The answer is that it leaves most of our citizens wondering whether we have a clear enough idea of what we mean when we accuse someone of being un-Australian in their behaviour toward others. We are quick to suggest that Aborigines should make up their minds on where they want to go and who they want to be within our diverse society framework, but we are left wondering whether the whitefellas and their migrant cousins have any clearer concept of their own identity and aspirational future.

Returning to the history of Christianity, our religion is easy to criticise on a range of earlier actions such as the Crusades, the Inquisition, the Slave Trade, colonial cruelty, and even the Holocaust. It also has the capacity to change with time, to abolish outdated practices and to adopt more humanitarian and tolerant doctrine and practice. The *Magna Carta* in Britain and the Declaration of Independence in America are examples of early humanitarian changes. Today, the constitutions of many modern democracies distinguish Western nations from both the totalitarian and the barbaric regimes of many Eastern cultures and theocracies. The difference between the largely-Christian and largely-Islamic cultures is writ large in both their open universities and their press freedoms.

The question right now is whether our education system in Australia has struck the right balance between comparative cultural values on the one hand and freedom of speech on the other. On the local scene, the extent to which Aboriginal culture and original identity can make a referendum case for constitutional change, should not be confused with the extent to which our socio-economic well-being stems from our Anglo-Christian-Humanitarian tolerance of difference and upholding of just principles. While many cultures may be equally defensible in their virtues, those at both ends of the continuum of values, are demonstrably not virtuously equal. So, while religious and patriotic fanaticism do conflict with general humanitarian values, our Constitution should reflect agreed global norms of productive, co-operative and socially-beneficial behaviour. The process by which a benign democratic legal framework is achieved requires that citizens be supported on the basis of need rather than of ethnicity.

Several policy advisors have suggested that the concept of 'race' is a socio-political construct and has no biological basis. This may be true scientifically, but among the great unwashed in voterland 'race' will probably remain very real, as reflected by appearance, language, religion, dress and ritual. To simply announce that we're doing away with race, i.e. no more races in Australia, seems almost bizarre in a nation born of its White Australia policy, and now known for its historic oppression of Blacks. So when groups of young men within the present mainstream decided to 'sort out the wogs' in the Cronulla riots, and more recently in similar 'Reclaim Australia' demonstrations, to re-take Australia, the easy-going bystander suffers at least mild schizophrenic uncertainty. He wonders whether or not he's doing enough about standing up for fair dinkum Aussie blokes and sheilas, or whether he should ignore the bogans and wogs and just have another beer while it all blows over as a harmless part of our cultural soup. The average suburbanite has seen it all before and intuitively knows that when testosterone-fuelled youths are doubly fuelled by alcohol, primeval urges are par for the course. Time to watch the footy.

THE FORGOTTEN PEOPLE:
Liberal and Conservative Approaches to Recognising Indigenous Peoples

Of all the glowing comments on this collection of fourteen essays published under the above title, the adjective 'timely' is the most apt. The editors, Damien Freeman and Shireen Morris, have made a sincere attempt to also give voice to Australia's right-wingers, since they have convinced themselves, correctly, that without conservative support the planned Indigenous Recognition Referendum will not be won. Many of us remember well how the last time we had a Constitutional Convention (the original Republic Con Con in 1998). It was about changing the Constitution to meet the requirements of a republic – a seemingly sure bet was lost through tricky wording of the questions in the ensuing Referendum in 1999. The proposal for a new preamble to the Constitution, put to the people at the same time, also failed.

Unsurprisingly, these two very well-informed editors give much credit to Noel Pearson and the Jewish legal fraternity for both originating most of the best Referendum proposals and driving the moving feast of Recognition proposals. Freeman and Morris deserve public acknowledgement for their personal commitment to Recognising Indigenous Australians in the Constitution. For at least two years there has been an on-going war of words about how best to ensure that the Referendum passes. All seem agreed that if the Recognition proposal were to fail, this would be a socio-political catastrophe which would set race relations back decades in this country.

After studying each of the essays, the reader becomes even more aware than they may have previously been, how the lack of agreed objectives of the Recognition process has largely been responsible for the shambles of the past three years. When every man and his dog was proposing more practical, more meaningful, more substantial, more acceptable, more legally valid and more fair modifications to the original recommendations of the Expert Panel in January 2012. After that date, the great unwashed voting public increasingly started to wonder whether there were any rules of engagement at all in this political hot potato.

Following collaboration with conservatives and liberals on the political right, Noel Pearson made the significant decision to shift his position in response to the political objections to the Expert Panel's proposal. Many of the essays pay tribute not only to Pearson, but also to ideas-people like Julian Leeser, Damien Freeman, Anne Twomey and Shireen Morris.

Part I of the book gives perspectives on the need for Recognition, while Part II compares symbolic with substantive Recognition proposals. The list of chapter authors makes for fascinating reading, as much for its omissions as its inclusions. A number of the essayists such as Chris Kenny, Greg Craven, Julian Leeser and Anne Twomey have been in this verbal duel since the onset, as has that wiley old sharpshooter, Malcolm Mackerras. To show the editors' even-handedness, Cardinal Pell and Lyle Shelton keep up the Christian end of the debate. Michael Jeffrey and Tim Wilson add breadth to the continuum of opinion. One would be excused if one suspected that those persuasive movers-and-shakers at Melbourne University Press may have made suggestions on who to leave out as authors. Some right-wing commentators have been conspicuously left out. Perhaps there is a perceived binary between nice and nasty conservatives, which leads to separating Cardinals and ex-Governor-Generals from the likes of Andrew Bolt and Gary Johns. The legitimate purpose of this book, however, is to showcase the conservative and liberal 'yes' case, and it does this persuasively.

All this background speculation pales into insignificance compared to the herculean task of getting Australian voters and political leaders to actually read this book. Several of the chapter authors mention two problems in achieving a positive Referendum outcome. The first is the challenge of getting the public to appreciate the significance of constitutional Recognition to Indigenous people and others who appreciate the real need for change. The second is the educational challenge of informing the public of the legal and moral logic of the proposed changes on which they will be asked to vote.

Since the Expert Panel's recommendations to the Prime Minister (three PM's ago) there have been numerous attempts to ignore, parody, defuse or otherwise derail the whole Recognition process. The reasons for this negativity are much the same as the first conservative responses to Native Title ('We'll all be rooned', as Hanrahan said). Claims of a hidden Bill of Rights, of self-government or independence or sovereignty (God forbid) or of a nation fatally divided, all resonated with the conspiracy theorists. Then came the opposing legal eagles who contested first the validity of changes to the Constitution and then suggested the possibility of achieving the objectives of Recognition elsewhere – in a Preamble, in poetic form, in a Treaty or in other documents. The list goes on. This collection proposes an alternative pathway forward that may be more capable of achieving the necessary political consensus.

This important book carries a much deeper and more subtle

message than just how to win the Referendum. It explores a range of unspoken sensitivities, including our historic guilt-hangovers and long-entrenched racial viewpoints, which the authors argue should now be abandoned. Many of the essays by non-Indigenous authors rekindle the old 'I'm not racist but...' discomforts of Australians who have a European history within an Asian geography. The more philosophical reader will note that some of the essayists have changed their minds on this issue over time. In this, there are parallels between many of these essays and the changes in popular opinion on issues such as smoking, gays, same-sex marriage, abortion and euthanasia. All took time, but tolerance and humanitarian values eventually won out. The present issue of Recognition by constitutional change via a Referendum is much more complex however, at least from a legal point of view. But this book offers hope that there is a way through.

It is a tad surprising therefore that the recent little volume, 'Everything you need to know about the Referendum to Recognise Indigenous Australians' (2015), by Megan Davis and George Williams doesn't get a mention by either the editors or the essayists. As a mini-encyclopaedia on the racial history of our Constitution, it's a doozy. Its persuasive reasons on why Australia's Constitution urgently requires updating would convince all but the most rusted-on conservatives. Included in that book is a masterful piece of sleuthwork by Williams in which he analyses, in great detail, how each of Australia's referenda were (mostly) lost, although one would have expected Williams to comment on how four Referenda scored exactly the same 'yes vote' of 49.3%.

The appeal for empathy and understanding of the psychological and material significance of substantive Recognition comes through best in Morris' chapter 'What promise will the nation make?' For the sake of brevity, clarity and balance, this particular piece warrants separate printing and distribution. Not only is it a magisterial summary of complexity, but it reflects an unusual grasp of both the legal and political implications of options proposed. Morris' appreciation of the deep understandings of Pearson, Twomey, Leeser and Freeman shines through. Behind the scenes, Morris has advised Pearson for several years and in this chapter she crystallises the insights of the other three in the boiler-room of constitutional change formulation.

Much of the present confusion in the public mind stems from the process used in the whole Recognise program. This process allowed members, including chairmen, of both the Expert Panel and the Parliamentary Select Committee, to gainsay their own group's recommendations, to agree to new proposals which contradict their recommendations and to submit new proposals. All these conflicting suggestions make a mockery of the $23m of taxpayer funds spent on the Panel. The absence of any agreed objectives and definition of Recognition, and clarity on how changes outside the Constitution could avoid having to hold a Referendum while achieving the required level of legal validity, now become glaring omissions.

'The Forgotten People' (based on Menzies' 1942 'forgotten class') is a valuable addition to Australian political history. Its logic touches on our reconciliation debate from the perspective of the political right, in a way that few other books do. In a quite unplanned way, this collection of essays provides us with a new window into the unreconciled facets of our nation's soul and suggests pragmatic ways for us to become more reconciled. For those in the 'Don't muck about with our Constitution' camp, Freeman summarises the situation by suggesting that there are overwhelming reasons for the Referendum to do just four things:

i.   Repeal section 25.

ii.   Amend section 51.

iii. Adopt a symbolic statement on the national significance of Indigenous people.

iv. Guarantee a non-binding legislative voice to these people.

Many in the mainstream may have thought that constitutional mention of three waves of migrants, of whom Indigenous people were the first, would have sufficed. But if, over the coming months of consultation, the First Peoples say they want a body to advise Parliament on laws affecting them, most Australians would probably have no problem with that. They no doubt thought that if the Constitution already states that all citizens are equal, special mention of one group would probably be unnecessary and confusing. It should be noted that the Adam Goodes simulated spear-throwing in front of the highly tribal MCG crowd has enlivened the Recognition debate in an important but largely confusing way, as indicated by several of the essayists.

Perhaps this review should finish by observing two important omissions in this book which, while not constitutional, are at the heart of who we are Recognising. The first omission is the validity of both the current Aboriginality test (three criteria) and the way in which it has been rorted for at least twenty years. More discussion is needed on whether this test is the most effective and efficient definition of Aboriginality.

The other omission is the lack of discussion on the extent to which a 3% minority should be catered for in a free democracy, irrespective of their origin. My own preference would be to guarantee that all citizens must be treated equally. If that proves politically unachievable, however, this book makes a strong case for reform to ensure that this 3% will always be heard.

WHY THE RECOGNITION REFERENDUM IS RIPE FOR SCARE CAMPAIGNS

Ever since PM Gillard established the Expert Panel on Constitutional Recognition of Indigenous People in late 2010, there has been on-going suspicion on both sides of the recognition debate that the acceptance of symbolic or substantive changes to the Constitution will unfairly privilege or disadvantage Indigenous people. Few have forgotten how the referendum on a republic was lost in 1999 as a result of scaremongering, confusion on the implications, and tricky wording of the referendum question. The fact that PM Howard convened a ten-day Constitutional Convention on the republic in February 1988, and the fact that several polls had previously reflected majority support for a republic, did nothing to bring the 'yes' vote near 50%.

By now we're probably all aware that only 8 of 44 referenda since Federation, have succeeded. That's not even 1 in 5. The very useful 'Everything you need to know about the Referendum to Recognise Indigenous Australians' (July 2015), by Megan Davis and George Williams of UNSW Law School, presents perhaps the best chronology of past efforts to change our Constitution. It appears to have pre-dated the more recent shenanigans of the period after September 2014, when several influential legal experts continued making late submissions to the Expert Panel on this matter, some making three or four different proposals spread over a three-year period.

Davis in particular, has made a detailed analysis of the repeated efforts by Aboriginal leaders to achieve recognition and equality through both a Treaty and constitutional change. Most scholars of Aboriginal policy would be aware of each of the building blocks in Davis' longitudinal study, but few would ever have seen these events so logically catalogued in historical sequence from 1788 to date. While there are instances of Davis and Williams' bias toward the Aboriginal cause, these in no way detract from the persuasive case made by them for substantive constitutional change. Their unpacking of the 1967 Referendum on the Aboriginal vote, reveals much which is not appreciated by the public at large, notably the 'new rights' that it *didn't* give Aborigines.

The general impression gained from this historic chronology, is a litany of bureaucratic mechanisms to avoid or postpone mandating equality under the law. They record the weasel words of every Prime Minister since Federation in their efforts to satisfy the mainstream voters while appearing empathetic to the Aboriginal cause. What is clear is the way the judgemental Darwinian view of different races has increasingly receded in the face of post-colonial knowledge of ethnic complimentarity.

Today's generation are probably unaware of the intensity of racism and white superiority which prevailed in 1901 when Federation was constituted. The White Australia Policy was implemented through language tests in European languages authorised by the Immigration Restriction Act 1901. Australia's first Prime Minister put it this way: There is no racial equality. There is that basic (=inherent?) inequality. These (tinted) races are, in comparison with white races…unequal and inferior.'

Barton compared the Englishman with the Chinaman, saying 'We see no prospect and no promise of this [deep-set difference] ever being effaced.' Barton was followed by PM Deakin who stated his vision for this 'Dark Continent' as: 'In another century the probability is that Australia will be a White Continent with not a black or even dark skin amongst its inhabitants. The Aboriginal race has died out in the South and is dying fast in the North and West, even where most were gently treated. Other races are to be excluded by legislation if they are tinted to any degree.' On the suggestion that Aborigines be given the vote, Isaac Isaacs, Australia's first 'native-born' Governor General was adamant: 'Aboriginal people have not the intelligence, interest or capacity' to vote. High Court Judge Henry Higgins too had no doubts: 'It is utterly inappropriate to ask [the Aborigines] to exercise an intelligent vote.'

It was in this spirit that the Constitution was drafted to exclude Aborigines, so it is unsurprising that Davis finds no evidence of any of her mob being consulted on 'the nation's birth certificate'.

All this cumulative detail on the call for equality by both Indigenous and non-Indigenous will do nothing to persuade the naysayers in the proposed 2017 Referendum, unless they are somehow informed of the facts. Ignorance and scare campaigns have never made for positive support in past referenda and this is unlikely to change.

In 2014, Williams and his colleagues published a detailed table of how each of Australia's past referenda fared, listing date, government, states approving and the total 'yes' vote percentage. This table makes fascinating reading and while there is probably a logical explanation, the average punter can be excused for suspecting something is amiss when they note that at least ten Referenda ended up with a 49% 'yes' vote. While Williams doesn't give the wording of each Referendum's question, the risk-averse

Aussie voter wasn't buying PM Howard's Republic question which asked us if we'd like a Republic in which the President would be elected by the parliament. Clearly the answer was, yes we want a Republic but no, we don't want the Head to be a politician's pick. Once again, the Dirty Tricks department won the day.

To avoid this trickery in the Recognition Referendum, Davis and Williams have a warning for naïve players in their chapter headed 'Myths and Misconceptions'. It is par for the course that exaggerations and misinformation form a constant element of contemporary politics. In the case of the Republic vote, the conspiracy theorists had a field day: Australia would be kicked out of the Commonwealth; Australia would need a new flag; the conversion process would cost $900M; we'd suffer a Hitler-like presidency and (horror of horrors) a Republic would allow Native Title over 'vast swathes' of Australia.

The list of emerging Recognition Referendum myths is difficult to compile right now, but the naysayers have about two years to build their case. To date, Davis informs us that the following dangers lurk: Recognition could lead to the imposition of Sharia law; Recognition could nullify Australia's anti-terrorism laws; Recognition would validate an Aboriginal Bill of Rights; Recognition would enforce Indigenous Law on our courts; Recognition would mandate a Treaty between Government and Aborigines; Recognition would legalise Indigenous sovereignty and independence; Recognition would cause unlimited claims for financial recompense for past dispossession of land, children, language and culture. Be assured that this scary list will grow longer. To the above negatives, the following could also be been added:

i. There are more important priorities for Government.

ii. Constitutional change is expensive.

iii. The Constitution has worked well; if it's not broke don't fix it.

iv. The High Court's interpretations could lead to serious unintended consequences.

v. There is no proven consensus on the changes required.

A relevant parallel case is the 2013 call for recognition of Local Government in the Constitution. To the LG proponents the case was clear: Australia has three tiers of government but only two are mentioned in our founding document. Surely this is illogical? So why was LG dropped? It was a dislocation. It was not the right time. It wasn't widely supported. Perhaps the Recognition Referendum awaits a similar brush-off, despite its sound logic.

Many Australians will be unaware that most States have been way ahead of the Federal Government on Recognition, at least as a symbolic gesture. Importantly, when State Parliaments recognise Aborigines as First People with special links to country, there is no need to change the Constitution or to hold a Referendum. Victoria was first to move on recognition in 2004 and was soon followed by Queensland, New South Wales and South Australia.

So far, so good; but the Indigenous view is not one of gratitude, but rather of disdain as a result of each of these States including what is termed a 'non-justifiability clause'. This means that recognition is symbolic only and has no legal standing, force or effect.

Three days before the 2007 election, when PM Howard was facing defeat, he announced that if elected he would hold a Referendum at an early date 'to formally recognise Indigenous

Australians'. This would 'ensure their special (though not separate) place within a reconciled, indivisible nation'. It appears that Howard had only consulted one Aboriginal leader – guess who?

Throughout this whole Recognition saga there has been a continuous argument about the inference of particular words: Howard's regret (vs sorry); Ridgeway's kinship (vs custodianship); Hawke's mateship (vs respect); Abbott's symbolic (vs substantial); Gillard's settlement (vs invasion); Rudd's advancement (vs benefit); and Pearson's drop the guilt (vs historic indebtedness).

There is no reference by Davis and Williams to the effect, if any, of race-mixing on the personality or capacity of the next generation. There is one mention of the 'fraught questions about when a person's ancestry means they are Indigenous' which comes up as a problem in drawing up a separate Indigenous electoral roll. I have examined the evidence of the link between skin colour and discrimination in my chapter '50 shades of Brown' ('Whitefella Dreaming', in press). The question at hand is the matter of genetic benefit to capacity, from infusion of DNA from a different group. My family's genetic profile for instance, is said to show remnants of Neanderthal, Viking, Celtic, Roman and Norman DNA. Similarly, 16% of white South Africans DNA can be attributed to the African group. So where should today's Aboriginal ancestral pride rest? Take the top twenty Indigenous leaders today; do they know who their forebears were? Have they checked their genetic profiles? Would they value their diverse heritage? Or would they continue with what Anthony Dillon, a proud part-Aboriginal, calls 'ancestral genocide'?

Rodney Dillon, a former ATSIC member and founder of Weetapoona Aboriginal Corporation in Tasmania which operates a sheep farm on Bruny Island, wants DNA tests to settle Aboriginality claims. This challenge is in response to Clyde Mansell, Chairman of the Tasmanian Aboriginal Land Council, who in early 2015 called for more rigorous testing to prevent being overrun by 'wannabe or tick-the-box' claimants. Mansell's discussion paper includes the requirement of 'a continual connection' with the community over generations, to eliminate the Johnny-come-lately claimants.

Rodney Dillon is adamant that Mansell's proposals are no more than a protection of established power groups who seek 'an elitist grip' on grant funds. The increase of registered Aborigines in Tasmania has risen sharply (by 17%) between the 2006 and 2011 census returns. In recent years, the number of regional Aboriginal organisations has risen to 19, all of whom are eligible for federal grants. Mansell claims that many of these are 'bogus' and need to have their Aboriginal credentials checked with established community groups. He suggests that proof of ancestry (by DNA) may be insufficient and he proposes a new test of continual connection with the Aboriginal community over generations. It is on these grounds that MP Jacqui Lambie's claim has been challenged by the TAC.

Rodney Dillon states in 'The Australian': 'Let's all have a test, then don't bother making out that you're Aboriginal.' Its foolproof and would prove once and for all who is Aboriginal. The present test used by Government and the First Peoples Congress is a three-part check on:

1. Aboriginal inheritance.
2. Activity in an Aboriginal community.
3. Acceptance by that community.

This test is problematic for those of the Stolen Generation who lost contact, not through choice but by force.

Davis tells us that: 'Some find it difficult to understand the connection between both poverty and disadvantage, and advocacy for institutional recognition.' Recognition and addressing discrimination in the Constitution is only *one of the things* that could be done to improve the situation (my emphasis). This has led me (Roberts, *Quadrant Online* 23/07/2015) to suggest 25 (other) things which warrant recognition. These suggestions have been met with accusations that my ideas were inflammatory and derogatory. This is a pity, because after much study of past policy failures it is clear to me that without recognition of many other aspects of our history and sociology, recognition of First People *per se* will not deliver the outcomes desired by the Indigenous leaders.

The concept of Indigenous 'Sovereignty' has been either avoided or treated with special caution by successive Federal Governments, but it remains a fact that substantive recognition of First Peoples would be by way of a sovereign-to-sovereign Treaty. Way back in 1832, George Arthur, Governor of Van Diemansland, claimed it was a fatal error that a treaty was not entered into. Even in 2000 the Corroboree Convention and the Council for Reconciliation concluded that a Treaty was a necessary part of Recognition. Treaties are usually only made between sovereign peoples or nation states. The US, Canada and New Zealand have done just that and it hasn't undermined either their Constitution or their structure as a nation. The problem of signing a Treaty is not a matter of constitutional power but simply of political will – like marriage equality.

Ever since 1835 when John Batman negotiated a Treaty between the settlers of Port Phillip in Victoria and the local Aborigines, and since G.A. Robinson negotiated his Oral Treaty with the Tasmanians, Government has repeatedly found reason not to continue these arrangements. One bright spot in these frustrating years was the 1977 formation of the National Aboriginal Conference (NAC) by PM Fraser. Justice Gibbs dismissed Paul Coe's claim to Aboriginal sovereignty in 1979, but Fraser's minister, Fred Chaney, pushed ahead suggesting that resistance to the term 'Treaty' might be overcome by the term *Makarrata*, meaning 'coming together after a struggle' in Yolngu. In his last days of office, Fraser established a Senate Standing Committee to examine the practicalities of a compact (Makarrata). It reported in 1983, recommending that Government consider such an agreement in consultation with the Aborigines. On taking office, PM Hawke abolished the NAC, 'reviewed' the Constitution and set up a framework for Land Rights.

In 1983, the Senate Committee recommended that a new anti-discrimination clause be added into the Constitution, but the clause only be implemented after a Treaty had been finalised. In the end, the Treaty was downgraded to the Reconciliation Campaign, reaching a climax with PM Keating's Redfern speech in which he acknowledged that whites took full responsibility for all forms of dispossession.

The contemporary informed citizen asks what the problem is with developing a Treaty. As with people's doubts about the implications of a 'yes' vote in the Recognition Referendum, there are similar fears of the unknown implications of a Treaty. Indigenous people would use the same reasons for a Treaty as for Recognition, but a Treaty would not require a change to the Constitution or a Referendum. PM Howard said that as a nation without sovereignty, Aborigines had no treaty power, which brought the debate back to sovereignty. That didn't please Yunupingu, Rubuntja and Dodson when they presented their bark Barunga Statement to Government in 1988, the year of the Bicentenary and Mabo. Barunga called for negotiation of a Treaty to recognise prior ownership, continual occupation, sovereignty, universal human rights and freedom. PM Hawke responded by promising a Treaty in that (1988) term of office. After 500 community meetings Government established ATSIC in 1989. Failing to honour his promise, Hawke was subjected to the humiliation of Yothu Yindi's song 'Treaty'.

Today, many of the Aboriginal leaders see constitutional change as a conspiracy mechanism to avoid a real Treaty which finally clarifies Aboriginal rights and powers. Without much more clarity on goals and purpose, be assured that the 2017 Referendum could be yet another ($45m) non-event. The good news is that every required corrective action on equality can probably be achieved legally without constitutional change.

The Referendum details will change again, but it is worth noting that at the end of March 2016 it was revealed that the Referendum Council (the body responsible for framing the Recognition Referendum questions) had put forward five options at its March 3rd meeting.

The original date of 27th May 2017 for the Referendum was first chosen as the 50th Anniversary of the 1967 Referendum on Aboriginal Citizenship. If Recognition can be achieved without changing the constitution, the costs of a Referendum will be saved. At its March meeting, the Council listed the following five options for the Referendum proposals:

1. A statement of Recognition of Aboriginal people, within or outside the Constitution, either as a Preamble or as a new Head of Power in the form of a Statutory Declaration of Recognition.

2. Reforming the Constitution's race power and removing

Section 25 and modifying Section 51 (26). (Agreement on the practical implications of the proposed wording will be crucial to interpretation.)

3. Creating a new Indigenous body to advise Parliament on laws affecting Aborigines.

4. Formulating ways of making binding agreements between Aborigines, governments and NGOs.

5. Guarantee against racial discrimination which binds parliament to equality under the law.

It is understood that #5 has since been deleted, and that #4 was added by Council itself. The Council had previously asked the Australian Institute of Aboriginal and Torres Strait Islander Studies (AITSIS) to submit budget estimates for carrying out community consultation at eighteen regional meetings and one national convention. These estimates came in at $9.8 million, revised down at Council's request to $7.5 million. AITSIS is chaired by Mick Dodson, brother of Patrick who recently resigned from the Council to take up a Labour Senate vacancy. AITSIS recommended that attendance at the proposed regional meetings would be on a ratio of 60:20:20 for First Nations rep's, Community Organisation rep's and key individuals (unspecified). These meetings would be convened by AITSIS.

The council itself was established in December 2015 and it is assumed that it has the responsibility of ensuring the wording of each of the referendum options is legal, clear and unambiguous. It is currently unclear whether voters will be asked to choose one preferred option or whether options are to be ranked 1-5 or some other preference selection method. Whether AITSIS's recommended 20% majority vote of First Peoples will apply to the meetings, remains to be finalised.

To the outside observer, the ability of the average voter to estimate the relative benefits of the competing options would appear to be near zero. One assumption is that the council will ensure that the strengths, weaknesses and implications for each option will be widely published in good time for voters to make informed choices. Because the issue is so legally complex, there appear to be several good reasons why it would be important for Council or the Expert Panel to publish their preferences plus rationale.

Many voters will be disappointed that a comprehensive explanation of the objectives of recognition has still not been spelled-out in terms of autonomy in various forms: self-determination, self-management, self-governance, independence or sovereignty. Others will regard none of the five options as capable of ensuring equality, non-discrimination or independence, whatever the legal wording of the referendum questions. Yet others will argue for replacing this whole illusory consensus with a Treaty. This group no doubt also hold that all except option #4 do nothing more than offer legalised 'feel-good' outcomes. If option #4 is paving the way for a treaty between two sovereign peoples, the wording should clearly reflect this objective. Word games on 'agreements' help nobody, except those trying to disguise their intent.

Finally, it should be noted that AITSIS is apparently not planning Indigenous-only regional meetings as had been proposed earlier by some Aboriginal leaders.

PART SIX
There is Only One Race

COMPARING AUSTRALIAN AND SOUTH AFRICAN RACISM

Introduction

Whenever race relations are debated, the authenticity of the commentators becomes an issue. I have lived half my life in South Africa and half in Australia. Having completed several degrees at an English-speaking university and having held a chair at an Afrikaans university, I migrated to Australia twenty years before Mandela's triumph in 1994. Since then, race relations in both countries have changed for the better and this essay compares those changes and their associated downsides.

The South African situation is unique in the way that the 80% Black majority of tribal peoples have taken over a modern industrial country. Australia's racial situation is unique in a different way, i.e. late colonisation by British Darwinists of one of the world's oldest and least developed tribal people, who today make up only 3% of Australia's population.

It is useful to remember that both the indigenous inhabitants and the invading colonisers were somewhat different in these two countries. The South African tribes were migrants from Central Africa (where *Homo sapiens* originated) whose economy was based on cattle and subsistence cropping. Their colonisers were first Dutch then British. The strong war-like Zulu tribes had caused the more peaceful tribes to flee south and north, where they came up against the British settlers and Afrikaans Voortrekkers respectively. The Australian case showed much less resistance from the indigenes, due largely to a combination of technical superiority of the colonisers and a lack of large-scale military organisation among the tribesmen.

This essay is one scholar's attempt to compare the racial situation in the two countries, informed by personal experience in Africa and comprehensive study in Australia. These writings draw heavily on contemporary writings of African and Aboriginal authors, as well as insights from European scholars on both continents.

While several issues are dealt with in some depth in these studies, three points stand out:

1. Skin colour is a poor indicator of genetic potential and thus of race.
2. The present requirements of a modern State cannot be met by the African National Congress's reversion to Zulu King-style governance under tribal chiefs.
3. Australian Aborigines should give realistic consideration to their communities' readiness to accept financial responsibility for democratic self-government not based on family structures.

Of particular significance in the South African situation is the way in which those Whites, Indians and Coloureds who voted for ANC's Rainbow Nation in 1994, now find that they have increasingly become marginalised to a status of powerless political minorities despite their commercial importance. Equally important in Australia, is the Aborigines challenge to position their group identity in such a way that it enhances their capacity to benefit from the modern well-being which arises from individual productivity within the worlds' most successful multi-culture.

It has become politically fashionable to join the call for a national 'conversation' on everything from domestic violence to mental health and racism. If this essay can contribute to the national debate on race relations, its purpose will have been served.

Background to Race as a Political Construct

Earlier research on the perceived differences between human races suggested that races could be separated by seven characteristics. During the past two decades, the way in which this classification had been used to construct a ranking of superiority, became seen as racist. This hierarchical arrangement of human groups was termed 'racialist' because of its romantic but non-biological treatment of race thinking.

The originator of this racialist (but not racist) view of human types was J.G. von Herder. His major (1780) work is titled 'Reflections on the Philosophy of the History of Mankind'. The writings of W.E.B du Bois, who became probably the most-quoted researcher on race in America, were very much influenced by von Herder's 'romantic racialism' and its nationalistic inferences. It should be noted that du Bois' most famous work, 'The Souls of Black Folk', has remained a seminal reference since it publication in 1903. A century later, Tommie Shelby published 'We Who Are Dark' (2005), subtitled 'Philosophical foundations of Black Solidarity'. This in turn is built on by Blum's own essay, 'Three types of race-related solidarity'.

Each of the above authors have made fundamental contributions to race identity which are of particular importance in understanding the Australian dilemma of group identity and its role in separatism and cohesion. At its root, the Aboriginal identity finds its grounding in three concepts: antiquity, colour and oppression. Each of these attributes is used in varying degrees to anchor Aboriginal solidarity. The idea that 'We are the First People, we are Black and we have long been oppressed' makes for a powerful togetherness and sense of belonging to a valued culture. No Whites can claim quite such a recent esteem-boosting background, and as such, may feel somewhat jealous of this pride-giving background.

Whatever the arguments about racial differences and indigenous groups, be they black, yellow or white, Blum lays it on the line when he claims that Indigeneity offers at least two distinctive characteristics which set them apart from invaders, colonists, settlers and migrants. These indigenous peoples are:

i. Genuine intergenerational 'collectives' characterised by distinctive social and historical experiences and (often) by socio-economic locations.

ii. Their socio-historical experiences are unique to the group and their self-image is (often) strongly influenced by the historical racist ideology applied to them externally.

While these two attributes of the generic indigenous group may seem bland and beg the question of 'what's new', they contain the seeds of Indigenous identity in a way that identity has never been described before in the Australian race debate.

Expanding on Blum's first characteristic of collective social and historical experience as a cohesive attribute, it is important to note that each member is inclined to identify with other members. In addition, the group is recognised as such by outsiders – they impress as a cohesive and different group of people. Their shared history and sociology confers on them a natural similarity which draws together all the strings of their fate as a collective. They may not always be aware of their biological linkage because it is instinctive and requires no conscious aggregation. So the group is much more than a mob who look alike; they are in fact the logical result of shared history, and in the Aborigines' case, a very long history unique in human development.

Blum's second attribute, distinct grouping on the basis of socio-historical experience, leads on to the realisation by Indigenes, that they are strongly influenced by the (unfounded) racist worldview applied to them by outsiders. Even the contemporary views experienced by Aborigines in the public square (or on SBS) reflect how intensely this superimposed self-image has affected senior spokespersons. They are aware that their past treatment at least reflected a disrespect for their assumed intelligence, as assessed by their oppressors, who justified their treatment on the basis of Darwinian science which suggested only sub-human evolution. The group's experience confirmed in their minds that they *were* a race, a collective, an aggregation of like individuals, all experiencing the same historical but inferior treatment as lesser mortals.

Blum points out that white racial groups are usually seen by outsiders as a social grouping, if not a biological one. He makes the telling point that people with the same skin colour (black or white) exhibit a wide range of different genetic features. This wide variation suggests that even if the colour group is not a biologically homogeneous *race* it is treated, through the racialisation process, as a *racial* group.

The South African situation post-1948 provided a case in point. Under Apartheid, groups were humiliated by the strict official recognition of racial categories. The discrimination and disadvantage which accompanied groups of darker complexion, caused racial self-identification to totally dominate each group's lifestyle and opportunities. So when Black Consciousness, Black Pride and eventually Black Power, gained the upper hand through democratic process, the whole ethos of group self-esteem took over and literally swept the dominating White minority aside.

Australians can learn from the way in which African peoplehood, in a historical sense, overcame the differences in individuals' experiential identity. This peoplehood stems from shared suffering and humiliation, which breeds solidarity and determination to improve group well-being. In a just world where equality is a serious constitutional matter, the need for group solidarity disappears. As Noel Pearson has pointed out, once the proposed Acts on equity have achieved their objectives, they can be removed from the required statute books in the Australia of the future.

Local intellectuals, keen to pursue the racial equity debate, frequently quote K.A. Appiah, a Ghanaian who shook the American race debate with his 1996 'Race, culture, identity; Misunderstood Connections'. Interestingly, Appiah's primacy of personal autonomy isn't shared by Blum, who considers group identity to be achievable and functional without the level of personal autonomy aspired to by Appiah. Because the positive and constructive character of racialised identity has its origins only in subordinated groups, who have been devalued by the dominant group's oppression, Blum believes there can never be a positive white racialised identity. I would disagree with this and have couched my arguments in a historic account of ancient English history, in which the indigenous Britons (First People) were invaded, subdued and enslaved by at least three different invading armies.

Australian Aborigines should be interested in the contemporary move away from non-racialism in contemporary South Africa. This view is well-expressed by Suran Pillay, an Indian writer from Cape Town. Pillay's experience is of an Apartheid in which racial divisions were all-encompassing; then of Mandela's Rainbow Nation (Tutu's term) in which races were constitutionally absent; then finally of the re-appearance of tribalism under President Zuma.

Somewhere along the continuum of ideologies between the tribal absolutists and the colourless pluralists, is a tolerant multiculture which not only respects difference, but builds on the richness of diversity. Pillay suggests that juxtaposing non-racialism against African Nationalism, as the only binary, is not a very bright idea. Similarly in Australia, the somewhat overblown Indigenous identity, promoted in the name of self-esteem of the formerly downtrodden, could probably do with a dose of Pearson's nuanced approach in his Quarterly Essay (2014) in which he seeks the answer to the Rightful Place of his people in a 'more complete commonwealth'.

The current Aboriginal leaders generally regard 'integration' as a dirty word, reflecting their unwillingness to be subsumed by the mainstream's values and customs. They are aware of many overseas examples of where the Indigenous minority's identity as a people, has been swallowed up by the dominant majority's education policy and the non-funding of their cultural preservation programs.

In this regard, it is useful to note the sentiments of Steve Biko, the promising young Black leader in South Africa who died after three days in police custody: 'At the heart of true integration is the provision for each man, each group, to rise and attain their envisioned self. Each group must be able to attain its style of existence without encroaching on or being thwarted by another. Out of this mutual respect for each other and complete freedom of self-determination, there will obviously arise a genuine fusion of the life-styles of the various groups. This is true integration.'

Is this also true of Australia?

In a compilation of essays, 'The Colour of our Future', by leading South African writers, the editor, Xolea Mangcu, subtitles her collected essays: 'Does Race Matter in Post-Apartheid South Africa?' She comes to the conclusion that it is by no means clear, as it once seemingly was, that: 'the great doctrine of 'non-racialism' is self-evidently the best way to engage and combat the scourge of individual and institutional racism.' This conundrum, which threatens the spirit of the Rainbow Nation (all colours equal), leads David Scott, the now-famous writer on modern racism, to proclaim in his Foreword to those essays: 'Unless we are able to deconstruct-reconstruct the conceptual-political story of race and ethnicity, we are not likely to come to terms with the uncanny persistence of race and ethnicity...'

In both South Africa and Australia, the Indigenous people must ask themselves whether the concepts and values which they so loudly proclaimed in the struggle against discrimination, help or hinder their cause once recognition and equity are achieved. In other words, the emphasis on past oppression and humiliation, both of which strengthened their feeling of peoplehood, may be less than helpful as guideposts in the transition of each nation to a truly pluralistic society in which (at least officially) the common good supersedes ethnic priorities and identities. Such reconsideration of previously-held truisms, on who we are, may repudiate some things which we have also always held to be true. This is never easy, but if it leads to the wider affirmation of new ways of seeing ourselves, the price of change will be repaid several-fold to future generations.

In the Australian situation, the early calls by Aboriginal leaders in the 1930s and 1940s virtually all reflected the same aspirations – a united nation in which there was no discrimination; equal opportunities for all; respect and tolerance; a fusing of the peoples, leading to a productive unified nation. The Whites at that time still suffered from Social Darwinism and exhibited a reasoned separatism based on what they clearly saw as distinct peoples who were at incompatibly different stages of development. While the Blacks may have been made to feel inferior by a wide range of discriminatory regulations, the early stirrings of a renewed sense of Aboriginal nationhood were clear to all who were willing to read the signs.

While still steeped in ancient tradition and responsibility to their ancestors, many of the early Indigenous leaders not only valued the benefits of modernisation, but were often, through their Christian persuasions, not averse to looking on an emerging Australian identity which downplayed the way in which they had previously been totally defined by their culture and its tribal values. The historic records repeatedly infer the presence of 'tame' and 'wild' Blacks, describing the former as progressive and the latter as degenerate – a depiction which was to be reversed in a few generations. By the 1980s the compliant 'Jacky Jacky' was branded, by his own people, as a turncoat abandoning his traditional duties. The Wild Black was converted in the emerging pride of First People, into the true ethnic role-model – the Absolute Aboriginal unsullied by the sins of the degenerate White man. Today he is epitomised by the likes of the Arnhem Land Yunupingus, proud to have survived two centuries of attenuated change by the invaders. As Elder, David Ross says: 'We just want to be ourselves; don't try to change us into someone we are not.'

Most attempts to justify racism, however benign, include a reference to the usual historic suspects: Darwin, Hume, Kant, Rawls, Hobbes, Weber, Marx, Hegel, and more recently du Bois, Sandel, Blumenbach, Blum, Appia, Falon and Fredrickson. By the simple expedient of first determining one's choice of heroes and villains, then selectively quoting from the list of 'authorities', well-referenced cases for both the 'for' and 'against' racist stances can, and have been, published with all the conviction of the open-minded, but unconsciously biased scholar.

Skin Colour

For a number of historic and psychological reasons, of all the attributes which are held to characterise 'the other', skin colour repeatedly stands out as the single most common indicator.

Since this became the basis for several 'Pigmentocracies', notably in South Africa, United States, Brazil and Australia, an understanding of skin pigment and its heritability is useful in unpacking the biology of colour. Nina Jablonski, an anthropologist from Penn State University, claims that skin pigmentation is the product of evolution by natural selection and as such, is one of the best examples of evolution acting on the human body. She regards skin colour as an ideal tool for teaching evolution. The second major outcome from her work is that: 'Similar skin tones have evolved multiple times independently in human history and [thus] *skin colour does not define human races* .' Jablonski is convinced that if this understanding of pigmentation is widely promulgated, it will not only assist in dispelling racism, but should discourage the 'repeated social invention of race as a political idea'.

Jablonski reminds us that Aristotle formalised the relation between skin colour and sunlight intensity (latitude) back in the fourth century B.C. Today we know that the pigment eumelanin (or melanin) is responsible for dark skin colouration. The ability to produce eumelanin has been shared by humans and our closest primate relatives for 1.5m years.

This pigment acts as a superior sunscreen and was present in the *Homo sapiens* population when they migrated from tropical Africa where the eumelanin protected their skin from the harmful effects of ultra-violet rays (UVR). Over time, *Homo sapiens* first lost their dense body hair, later their dark skin, resulting in a continuum of colour from the Equator to the Arctic Circle. Modern humans have been living in the Tropics for over 60k years and in high latitudes (>50 degrees) for approximately 40k years. These new low UVR environments caused a reduction in the body's ability to produce vitamin D. This in turn, resulted in lower eumelanin which allowed higher vitamin D production. Recent studies indicate that somewhere along the evolutionary track, a specific genetic mutation occurred which led to de-pigmentation in the ancestors of today's Western Europeans. Strong natural selection had probably acted to establish de-pigmented skin as the normal appearance of people at high latitudes.

Skin de-pigmentation is thus a Darwinian adaptation, i.e. through evolution by natural selection. However, skin colour, according to Jablonski, is *not* a useful trait for separating people into unique groups. Despite the fact that skin colour was used for centuries to define human races, it is an inappropriate measure, since skin tones are not unique. It is thus of the greatest importance for potential leaders and sociologists to recognise that racial classification based on skin colour is totally unjustified. The prime reason for this is that skin pigmentation evolved independently of other physical and personality traits.

Historically-implied Racial Traits

For at least a couple of centuries the following features were regarded as characteristic of racial groups, sufficient to refer to them and treat them as 'races':

1. Each race exhibited mental and psychological characteristics specific to their group.
2. These qualities were rooted in the group's biology.
3. These qualities were passed on generationally through genetic inheritance.
4. The differences between races were fixed and thus unchanging biologically.
5. The races differed in skin colour, eye shape, hair texture and facial features.
6. The races originated in specific global regions.
7. By a combination of the above six features, races could be ranked from superior to inferior.

This classic racist ideology stood for many years and still persists in some societies. Although it was externally imposed, today there is an additional (positive) internal imposition of racial difference, by those modern tribalists who see pride and solidarity in racial separatism.

In both South Africa and Australia this tribal pride is exhibited by emerging movements seeking an enlivened historic identity as a counter to multiculturism, pluralism and a perception of loss of an innate sense of tribal belonging. Because the issue of personal identity is primarily emotional, rather than factual, governments of mixed-race nations are loath to recognise that racialised groups can embrace a positive personal identity.

In South Africa, the negative connotations of racial categories are so deeply embedded as a hangover from Apartheid that most citizens believe that such divisions should be entirely discarded. In this climate of non-racialism, the emergence of a strong tendency toward clearer Zulu or Xhosa tribal identity has disappointed those who were relying on the new Constitution (1994) to carry the united banner for a true multiculturism.

In Australia the situation is similar but different. Tribal or clan identity has emerged as the basis for self-esteem, respect, pride in ancestors, links to country and the case for compensation or at least restitution of land ownership. As a result, policy-makers are grappling with the means by which national coherence and unity can be achieved without losing the personal pride which drives group members as productive individuals.

There is a demonstrable power that arises from shared negative experiences of oppression, which strengthens affiliation and the common cause. In the Australian case, the 3% minority status of Aborigines is so different from the South African +80% that Aborigines' 'perceived powerlessness' has caused them to seek a proud identity, not in national citizenship, but in family and in home country – the only place they perceive to attain recognition, belonging, respect and an absence of discrimination. This tribal identity has complex problems for the 80% of urban-dwelling Aborigines. The 'us and them' ideology of ethnic recognition does little to encourage a feeling of national unity. For the Aboriginal cultural purists, group justice far outweighs national cohesion, to the extent that some extremist leaders denounce their Australian identity as being at odds with who they really are, or want to be. Racial justice leaves social harmony as a very poor second priority.

Non-Racialism as an Ideology

David Everatt is a historian of non-racialism and has produced 'The Origins of Non-racialism: White opposition to Apartheid in the 1950's' (2009). This work compares what Chapter 1 (Section 1) of the South African Constitution states on non-racism, with what is rapidly emerging in the increasingly tribal African National Congress, which is the real policy formulation centre of the country. Everatt states that in contemporary South Africa the concept of non-racialism has as many meanings as there are spokesmen. Neville Alexander's 'Thoughts on the New South Africa' (2012) however, makes a bold attempt to unpack this complex concept, suggesting that separate elements of non-racialism require individual assessment. These elements are summarised by Blum (2015) as four inter-related subjects:

1. Racial justice.
2. Eliminating inequality between classes (rather than races).
3. Race identities as tainted by Apartheid.
4. Race as an unnecessary category in a transformed modern nation.

Alexander shows how Black Empowerment and Affirmative Action have allowed a growing number of the African majority to rise economically above the poverty line. This has led *class* rather than *race* to be the new measure of well-being.

In Australia, the earlier ambition of a non-racial society has been replaced by a new Aboriginal desire to develop and maintain a proud group identity, while expecting the amended Constitution (2017?) to cope with a more equitable distribution of wealth to the First People.

Path Dependence: A New Concept for Australia

In 1990, D.C. North came up with the term 'Path Dependence' in his book 'Institutions, Institutional Change and Economic Performance'. With the exception of S.E. Page's 'Path Dependence' paper (2006) this concept appears to have had limited exposure, but it may well hold useful principles for both South Africa and Australia.

North's contention is that our patterns of the past persist as dogged determinants of our future, i.e. that different peoples somehow call on their previous group experience to control or at least guide, their consideration of alternative ways of meeting the future. North wanted to find out why some societies were able to achieve and maintain high productivity and well-being, while others, with seemingly similar resources, stagnated and never progressed above subsistence level. North's Path Dependence does explain why, twenty years after the demise of Apartheid in South Africa, the social hierarchies of that era still persist.

Perhaps North could explain why many Australian Aborigines apparently have such difficulty in adopting modern societal norms. North points out that for a society in transition, say from tribal rural settings to the multicultural urban environment, their past is not destroyed but rather is transcended. Steven Friedman of Rhodes University, South Africa, uses the above transcendence concept in his chapter 'The Janus Face of the Past' in the book 'The Colour of our Future' (2015) in which he also contrasts the cases for and against Path Dependence, a debate so crucial to South Africa's future as a social democracy.

Sustainable advances in societal well-being, in Friedman's view, are achieved by retaining aspects of the past which are of value, while moving beyond those aspects which would not contribute positively to the planned future. The primary reason for using Path Dependence as an explanation of differential progress between different societies is that, as a concept, it can actually identify which elements of society and its norms remain constant while significant change is happening. In this way, Path Dependence can demonstrate if and how the transitioning society is (or isn't) on a path that repeats past patterns which were the basis of that society before change was brought about by the political majority.

This question of how much traditions or previous norms form a well articulated element of our future is one which has been heard long and loud in the Aboriginal context as well. Put another way, to what extent should we allow our next generation to be defined by past patterns and values? On this issue, the majority of both Australian and South African Indigenes find themselves 'with a vote but no voice' as Friedman puts it.

Of course sceptics will say that North has done no more than given a name (an inappropriate one at that) to the long-recognised truism that humans tend to repeat those patterns embedded in their psyche by their past – a phenomenon which has previously been referred to by many names. While this is generally true, North's 'Path Dependence', as applied to the South African situation, has a few note-worthy messages for today's Aboriginal policy-makers.

Path Dependence can be seen in many aspects of our contemporary societies, our social connections, cognitive structures and even in our behavioural routines, all of which exhibit the way that our past is still well represented in our present. In the same way, historic patterns of group domination can still be seen in multicultural countries such as Australia.

The politics of power and how it has given moral gravitas, applies in both South Africa and Australia. In the former country, as Friedman points out: 'The moral difference between Afrikaner nationalism's triumph in 1948 and the end of Apartheid in 1994 are huge. The Afrikaners were rebelling against a century and a half of British colonialism, but in coming to power their prime goal was to prefer White Afrikaner dominance at the expense of the Blacks' majority.' In Australia the Blacks' struggle was against White colonial dominance of their dispossessed minority.

Today the South African majority seek only the full application of the intent of their new non-racial Constitution, while in Australia the minority seek a changed Constitution which recognises their place in the nation. The moral power in both cases lies with the oppressed.

In South Africa, the cohesion of the two White language groups guaranteed a Path Dependence which lasted nearly half a century, up to 1994's Independence. By this time only 1% of Whites lived in poverty while virtually all Blacks had been poverty-stricken for generations. The Australian situation is similar, but not so intense. The Aboriginal moral claim is primarily one of original land ownership; the Black African claim is simply rule by the majority. However, the South African Whites had viewed the Western democracies as their role model, leading to the new republic's double Path Dependence, i.e. parallel historical patterns of the two major political groups. Today the Zuma-led government is in real danger of inadvertently reverting to Apartheid patterns of tribal chieftains, with homelands ruled by Zulu King-type monarchies.

This autocracy of strong families also looms large as a threat to social democracy in Aboriginal homelands where decision-making is often the sole prerogative of the 'Big Men' and their families. At this level, the lack of financial accountability for public funds is problematic in both countries. In Australia it is less serious because of the small scale of corruption relative to the national budget. In South Africa the enormous scale of corruption reflects how tribal Path Dependence can bring the whole nation dangerously close to becoming a failed state.

So today in South Africa, in Friedman's words: 'The national debate is framed as a critique of the post-1994 (Independence) governance in general and the misdeeds of the ANC in particular; explicitly or implicitly, the debate insists that current difficulties are the consequence, not of deep-rooted problems whose origins be embedded in the [Apartheid] past, but in the misdeeds of the governing party and its leadership since 1994.' This situation diverts the debate away from the obvious need for changed government priorities. This is a clear manipulation of Path Dependence, as demonstrated by the ruling party's absolute refusal to recognise, and admit to, that dependence. Rather than government changing policy to include presently-excluded beneficiaries of government largesse, the powerbrokers argue about who of their number of elites should receive a greater share of the looted public purse.

The Australian parallel may be seen as somewhat tenuous, but here too the Aboriginal Fat Cats thrive on taxpayer funds while the remote homelands continue their Fourth World existence. In both countries, the women have had enough of fending for themselves as the torch-bearers of family dignity, and are defying the Big Men's irresponsible behaviour, by demanding not only a place at the decision-making table, but a gender meritocracy which better reflects the required integrity of their mob's decision-makers, notably at local level.

Both of the countries referred to here need to chart a new path toward greater inclusion of minorities, in which all voices are not only heard, but are given the opportunity to equitably participate in the widely-spread distribution of wealth. In South Africa's case, reverse discrimination based on historic, unconscionable neglect by Whites, is everywhere to be seen. In Australia's case, despite legal equity, Indigenous Australians remain seriously disadvantaged in job-seeking and housing applications.

The South African situation has no option but to respond to the dire economic threats of Path Dependence. As a nation, its borrowing rights are already seriously constrained and unless the present tribal nepotism is curbed, economists and sociologists see out-migration as the only hope for progressive individuals. Australia's challenge is not economic but rather it is moral and cultural. A racially guilt-laden nation with doubts about its own multicultural identity, could possibly find a spiritual grounding in ancient Indigenous values which, if constructively applied, could strengthen the cohesion which is presently deficient.

Constitutional Non-racism

Australia is trying to follow South Africa's non-racial Constitution in a way which specifically recognises Aborigines as the country's First People. The South African 'rainbowism' (Bishop Tutu's aspiration) seems to disregard the well-known fact that social action is driven essentially by self-interest. This results in alternating moods of euphoria and despair among the masses when they realise that human's material acquisitive nature, too-often over-rides the aspirational moral high ground.

South Africa as a nation, actually started its existence as a Federal Union of four provinces (states) which applied qualified franchise for both White and Black voters from its foundation in 1910 up until 1931. When educational and financial voting qualifications were dropped, and Blacks were moved to a separate roll, African women suffered from what Joel Netshilenski of the Johannesburg Institute for Strategic Reflection, calls 'triple oppression' – as Blacks, as women and as workers. This hierarchy of oppression is not too different from the situation in which today's urban Aboriginal women find themselves. The chances of the amended Constitution rectifying their situation are probably small in both countries.

Some argue that multiracialism easily becomes *racialism multiplied* in practice. The Pan African Congress (PAC), a conglomerate of anti-colonial African organisations, never regarded multiracialism as its ideal. On the contrary, its first president Robert Sobukwe, did not promise rights to any minorities. His was, as a paraphrased US president once said, *for* Africans, by a government *of* Africans and *by* Africans.

Whether some Aboriginal constitutional lawyers also harbour an exclusiveness in their call for recognition, is not clear. Certainly they seek self-government, but just how they perceive their aspirational separatism is yet to be articulated. There is a sameness about their independence calls to those of the South African ANC, who in 1994, organised to mobilise all the local Africans who had suffered dispossession and oppression. It sought to build national (Black) confidence and to use its new-found pride, as a political majority, to become not only assertive, but to make-up for lost opportunity without delay.

This racially-based self-esteem and group pride notion, is a central plank of Aboriginal aspiration, a goal which their leadership believes can come from constitutional changes. In both countries, the Whites (as taxpayers and employers) were expected, even obliged, to actively contribute to correcting the wrongs of the past. After all, they were the beneficiaries of cheap labour, land acquisition and a servile workforce.

Because the racial ratios are so different, Australia cannot expect to repeat the South African miracle of transition which happened peacefully, against all predictions, in 1994. The general indicators of progress toward greater national well-being (which includes the former dispossessed) are probably similar in both countries. These include measures of health, education, employment and housing. In addition, they include freedom of speech, religion and other human rights. However, evaluation of the measures of national pride, social cohesion and tolerance, continue to baffle the politicians as necessary adjuncts of well-being. The role of the State, vis-a-vis the responsibility of the individual, in gaining equity in wealth distribution, remains a highly politicised issue for peoples in transition.

After twenty years of constitutional racial equality in South Africa, unemployment is still 27% among Blacks and 7% among Whites. Income, housing and tertiary education reflect similar differences. In Australia, such inequities led to nation-wide calls to 'Close the Gap'. Indigenous spokespersons, such as Stan Grant, have recently (December 2015) received praise and brickbats for publicly claiming that Aboriginal Australians are 'far from free'. Grant uses the statistics on infant mortality rates, incarceration rates, suicide rates, child abuse rates, substance abuse rates and domestic violence rates, to demonstrate that actual opportunities for Aborigines are vastly different from those enjoyed by mainstream Australians.

These disadvantages are the product of a racist agenda which is shared by too many people, in Grant's view. While he acknowledges that Indigenous communities 'need to do more' (for themselves), he claims that simply acknowledging two centuries of wrong toward his people will help their communities to work toward healing themselves. Grant's claim that the 'Australian Dream is built on racism and bigotry' is probably rejected by many who recognise a range of causes of the Aborigines' present state of well-being. The same goes for Grant's claim that the Aboriginal 'underclass' is caused by factors such as unemployment, poor health and abuse. We need to look at the origins of these causes.

In South Africa the out-migration of heavily-taxed Whites and Indians makes closing 'The Gap' a somewhat nebulous concept. South Africa has to deal with additional complications, such as the Apartheid categories of Indians and Coloureds, who today exhibit considerably greater entrepreneurship than the African majority.

The 2011 South African statistics reflect this differential capacity in the poverty percentages of different ethnic groups. The income poverty line was set at R 620/month (AUD$62) per adult. Applying this definition, revealed that no less than 54% of Africans lived below that line, while the comparative figure for Coloureds was 28%, for Indians 3%, and for Whites 1%. Unsurprisingly, the envy of Africans is not limited to achieving the Whites' position, but to matching other groups who also achieve at a higher rate.

Constitutional change in any country, can do little about the fact that racism is a social construct and cannot be effectively legislated against. Illustrative of the societal basis for racism, is the way in which kindergarten children act in a manner which has become known as 'colourblindness', where children of all races play happily together. However, by the time these same kids reach their teens and enter high school, racial discrimination is often easy to detect and difficult to counter.

Incompetence and Tolerance

Whenever oppressed people are given new opportunities to enjoy equity and full recognition, the initial stages of transition usually include special programs to favour those who were formerly discriminated against. In this process, the maintenance of performance standards and efficiency in the job market can become a major economic problem. In the New South Africa, where early job creation was so crucial, when private enterprise couldn't afford to employ unskilled newcomers, the government stepped in and created millions of civil service and government agency positions. Predictably, the inability of the new occupants to carry out the required tasks was compounded by the lack of actual public service commitment by the ANC government.

The Australian situation is very different since the Aboriginal population only makes up 3% of the population. The need to educate and upskill the new generation of employees has led to the introduction of many different training schemes, albeit with mixed results. In tertiary education, Australian universities have been accommodating, giving special dispensation to some, but not all, the Aboriginal students who have shown the initiative to advance their self-improvement. Understandably, many of the programmes in Aboriginal homelands had less than satisfactory outcomes for the communities concerned. In many cases a lack of both financial accountability and commitment to the common good (beyond the dominant family), resulted in poor investment of government funds.

In both countries referred to here, the tolerance of taxpayers is sorely tested when the extent of incompetent economic management reveals significant wastage. Compassion, or at least empathy from employers, for those left behind in terms of well-being, clearly has its limits, especially when highly-taxed small business operators are having a hard time financially.

In the South African case, the economic situation is serious enough to affect the country's IMF borrowing rights. In Australia, as referred to earlier, the issue is more moral than financial. The need to encourage economic self-sufficiency deserves continued high-level support. In both countries, the government's decision on weighing the motivation and initiative of individuals against the effects of past victimhood, needs honesty and consideration of fair dealing for both transitioning peoples and taxpayers. This means calling out irresponsible attitudes, be they poor work ethics, dereliction of duty, plain incompetence, lack of will or disrespect for others.

In South Africa, many business observers foresaw what they termed 'Black incompetence' as a potential threat to the running of an advanced industrial economy. The need for maintenance of White expertise and business acumen were seen as an essential factor in political transition. Two generations was regarded as a realistic period for Blacks to take their rightful place in the economy, but in its haste to live high on the hog, the ANC government has ignored the basic laws of Keynesian economics and has put the entire financial security of the State at risk.

I have elsewhere described a fictitious new Aboriginal nation's predicted problems with economic management of their hard-won home country 'Aboriginalia'. In this futuristic scenario, the past record of Aboriginal money management is used to demonstrate how tribalism and a lack of economic vision can lead to sovereign bankruptcy. The demise which is depicted in this scenario, is the result of a basic lack of personal responsibility and an unrealistic expectation of what Noel Pearson has referred to as a labour-free income. When greed and ostentatious behaviour combine with sheer incompetence on the part of power-brokers, the common good loses out and the masses suffer.

Australia is unlikely to experience the same intensity of this combination of negative attributes, but the potential for a new nation of First Peoples to commence down this slippery slope is not at all beyond possibility. The way in which South African freedom fighters have rapidly lost the moral high ground when given two decades of political power holds lessons for other Indigenous groups seeking their own version of *Uhuru* (freedom).

Civilisation – A Neglected Concept?

Netshitenzhe (2015) reminds us, once again, that the attributes of a civilised society, as demonstrated over millennia, not only bear re-examination, but are forgotten at the peril of emerging societies. He suggests that the five characteristics of a civil society are:

1. The ability to master the laws of nature and advance scientific endeavour in the service of humanity.

2. The development of social and political relations underpinned by generations of human rights such as political freedom, social equity and protection of the environment.

3. The operation of social mores founded on integrity and compassion in individual and social relations.

4. Respect for the individuality of each person as a member of the human family, allowing the human spirit free rein.

5. Global interaction through peaceful and equitable relations between peoples, each enriching the other.

These attributes of a civilised society bear re-consideration whenever old-fashioned tribalism rears its head. It is also useful to consider anti-colonial struggles against the values embedded in the above measures of civility. In both South Africa and Australia, these values were largely, but not completely, met by the colonising governments. While opposing views will be held on the degree of civil behavioural norms achieved in each nation, there is a danger that 'progress' is too often assessed in 'techno-physical bean-counter' measures. The liberation movement and their freedom-fighters might be excused from being so focussed on liberty and equity that they neglect to elucidate a clear vision of what their victory might actually lead to, by way of their envisaged Utopia and its values. At the same time, it is perhaps not surprising that there is often no clarity on exactly what it is that such Utopians seek to achieve.

One of the problems for newly-liberated societies is what has been referred to as the 'sins of incumbency', i.e. putting self-advancement before service to the public. Accompanying such lack of integrity is the new regime's tendency to attempt to remain in office through generous patronage, commonly called vote-buying.

This process of self-aggrandisement is well described in Frantz Fanon's 'The Wretched of the Earth' (1961) which explains how this phenomenon, so common in Africa, is heavily reliant on an uneducated populace. President Zuma's pre-election hand-out of food parcels to poverty-stricken rural voters is a clear indication of patronage at work among the uneducated, at the same time as Zuma was found guilty of spending millions of treasury funds on his extravagant home complex in Zululand (officially promoted as a fine example of rural development).

Return to Racism

As referred to earlier, racial identification as a source of pride and self-esteem, has gone full circle since South African Independence in 1994. It is informative to examine how the much-touted non-racism of the new Constitution has now been overtaken by an enlivened racism based on the reinstatement of tribal chiefs and the re-introduction of tribal law in the rural homelands. Whether Australian Aboriginal leaders would ever revert to serious appreciation of 'non-racism' after two decades of emphasis on tribal identity and mother country, remains to be seen.

The Australian Aboriginal pride of origin probably stems largely from a feeling of failure to gain respect from outsiders, with the result that a sense of belonging is sought internally. Had Aborigines enjoyed acceptance and respect as genuine 'mates' in the Australian context, the current reversion to tribal identity as a means of discovering a sense of belonging, would probably not have become so intense. Many observers would contest this assertion, but the evidence from many successful integrated Aborigines is that those who felt accepted only belatedly joined the trend of publicly announcing that they are proud clansmen.

As referred to in the earlier section 'Background to Race', the South African reversion to racism is well described by Suren Pillay in his 'Why I am no longer a Non-Racist: Identity and Difference' (2015). Pillay is a South African Indian at the University of Western Cape, originally established for mixed race 'Coloureds' under the Apartheid regime. His powerful essay aims to determine whether non-racism (as mandated under the Rainbow Nation's Constitution) is a useful concept in planning South Africa's political future, rather than whether it's a good or bad idea ideologically.

Pillay draws on two ideas put forward by the British Jamaican

Stuart Hall, namely 'Conjuncture' (coming together) and 'Strategy' (how we organise and sequence change). Pillay asks whether non-racialism as an ideal actually achieves the objective of finally ridding the country of Apartheid's racial categories of African, White, Coloured and Indian (Asians were pooled with Coloureds). His arguments come from Black Consciousness thinkers who regard 'blackness' as a form of group solidarity, derived from their shared experience during 'the struggle'. In this way, blackness is no longer a racial category but a social identifier.

In the same way that Noel Pearson proposes that Australian policy-makers drop the concept of 'race' altogether, non-racialism in South Africa was also meant to strengthen the idea that there is only one race – the human race. In both countries, politicians appear confused about the merits of non-racism as understood by sociologists in the past few decades. In South Africa, there is a clear re-racialisation in the public square to the extent that the ANC, and its Zuma-led government, hardly disguise their aspiration for an African government in which minorities would play an insignificant (if any) role. The race-bred consciousness of the Apartheid years would morph into a purist African nation reminiscent of the early Zulu kingdom of the 1800's.

While such tribal dominance is of great concern to progressive democrats, sheer numbers don't auger well for the millions of non-Africans and it brings up the possibility of a second Apartheid era by another name. The Australian situation presents, not a parallel case, but an example of integration without loss of group identity in which individuals are invited to accept that they are first and foremost Australians.

Pillay ponders whether the replacement of White racism by Black racism actually has more merit in an emerging African nation which is strongly dominated by one race. In this consideration, the race/clans nexus becomes important. In Australia, many authors including the present one, have proposed that welfare policy be moved from a racial base to a *needs base*. No more ticking the box for 'Aboriginal' for health, education, housing and business loans, but rather the assessment of well-being indicators to identify 'need categories' only, irrespective of ethnicity.

In both countries, there is a strong case to move the political debate from racial categories to class categories. In South Africa, there is an antagonism between non-racialism and the more recent government emphasis on African Nationalism. The contemporary political balance between city and rural voters shows a clearly increasing dissatisfaction with the ANC government in all urban areas. This has caused Zuma, as frontman for ANC tactics, to enact all manner of regulatory support in shoring up his rural base by a return to rule by tribal chiefs. Those pre-election food parcels epitomise this desperate shift to enhance electoral chances.

David Everatt questions the ANC's capacity to run a genuine democracy in his country. Everatt maintains: "It remains questionable whether that same (Rainbow) African National Congress is about to throw off the constraints and racial blinkers of nationalism and truly embrace non-racialism." The question must now be asked whether Black dominance will lead to what has been termed 'Internal Colonisation', in which the ruling Africans force their culture and values onto their population's minorities, who may be segregated geographically in proscribed urban locations.

In a minority situation, many Aborigines support a similar separation of homelands, but they seek a separateness which preserves culture and racial identity (by another name) and is self-governed. The extent to which these 'sovereign' entities are to remain reliant on the Australian taxpayer is unclear, as is their contribution to federal tax income. The desire for self-rule, in its various forms, is a global phenomenon reflecting humans' innate tendency to seek a sense of freedom and belonging. Problems arise when peoples within one nation state seek independence within or outside the state's monetary system. History shows that independence is never given, but has to be taken, so when such ethnic nationalism rejects non-racialism entirely, as is the case with the South African 'Economic Freedom Fighters' party, the very essence of social democracy is lost.

While the popularity of 'Africa for the Africans' must be reckoned with by policy-makers who value national cohesion in South Africa, the Australian Aboriginal chant of 'We Demand our Land Back' has more moral imperative than economic justification. As an alternative to separation, Steve Biko, the assassinated pre-independence Black leader in South Africa, left us with his view of a well-assimilated nation. This view warrants repeating (again): 'At the heart of true integration is the provision for each [individual] and each group, to rise and attain their envisaged self. Each group must be able to attain its style of existence without encroaching on or being thwarted by another. Out of this mutual respect for each other and complete freedom of self-determination, there will obviously be a genuine fusion of the lifestyles of the various groups. This is true integration.'

This positive view of multicultural integration probably receives wide support from minorities everywhere. There are however, notable exceptions, and these are mostly ethnic groups whose religion or antiquity affect their willingness to adopt majority lifestyles which they regard as culturally inappropriate. As a result, the public assessment of these folks as unbending, old-fashioned, fundamentalist, ultra-conservative, unadaptive, isolationist or primitive, does little to encourage their integration.

In Australia, the Aboriginal population (self-identified) displays a continuum of degrees of integration, as described by Biko. Similarly, in South Africa, there is widespread support for an integrated non-racial multiculture, but for reasons of political survival, the present ANC government fans the flames of an exclusive African nationalism. In this political climate, democratic tolerance comes a poor second to popular promises of ethnic preference for the majority. The outcome of this shallow political ploy is that it destroys the nation's chances of embracing difference and the benefits of cultural enrichment which stem from diversity.

The political alternatives to Apartheid were never well thought through, and when majority rule finally came, the overwhelming realisation of 'freedom at last' so dominated the early euphoria that more nuanced non-racialism was nowhere to be seen. In crude terms, the time had arrived to settle old scores, to make up for lost time, and even time for 'payback'. Given the recent horrific history of Apartheids' inhumanity to Non-Whites, empathy for the Afrikaans losers was also nowhere to be found in the new Black South Africa. Under these circumstances, and after the justified international lionising of Mandela as the ultimate freedom fighter and champion *par excellence* of the oppressed, it seems trite to suggest that Apartheid in its original meaning of 'separate development' could actually have formed the basis of a peaceful and productive nation state.

However, even before the raft of cruel discriminatory laws were introduced, the basic decision to allocate only 16% of the nation's land area to over 80% of the population, set the scene for an unworkable political plan. There was also no intention of dropping the master/servant relationship as a basis for labour supply.

Pillay, in a critique of the unsustainable economic and racial position which South Africa has got itself into, maintains that the real solution lies in generating a pragmatic third option to the current simplistic choice between non-racialism and Black Consciousness. His contention is that 'Left to drift, [political] difference denied, might translate into the politics of difference demanded'. In the process, the deracialised civil society would become confronted by an 'ethnicised' political elite, who play the shallowest of popular political games with their gullible constituents. Since cheap politics thrives on ignorance, and the key to a maturing South Africa depends on the educated voters and the growth of professionalism, it is worth examining professional educational trends in South Africa.

Higher Education's Essential Role

It is well understood that the quality of graduates depends largely on the intellectual capacity, literacy and numeracy of the school-leavers who enter the tertiary system. The former Deputy Vice Chancellor of Cape Town University, Crain Soudien (2015) has published arguably the most incisive insider's account of the way local universities have transitioned over twenty years of independence. While the expectations of universities is to produce the informed human capital required to drive the economy, the rush to prepare a new Black managerial class has caused real problems with academic standards. At the same time, the tertiary enrolments tell a complex story.

Over the period 2000-2010, the average annual enrolments of the five major racial groups are:

- Africans 6.5%
- Coloureds 6.8%
- Indians 3.3%
- Whites 0.9%.

(The latter two groups are increasingly seeking their tertiary education overseas.)

Like most intellectuals writing about the role of the university, Soudien quotes Max Weber and (of course) Cardinal Newman (1854), the latter making the point that an essential attribute of a good university is that as an institution it is *open*, meaning both students and staff are as diverse politically as the populations that they came from. Every kind of knowledge from every type of culture had a place in such an organisation. In addition, universities were at their best when they not only conserved the accumulated knowledge and transmitted this to their students, but also created new knowledge. Overall, enlargement of the mind, through exposure to openness of diverse knowledges, was Newman's noble objective.

Theoretically, South African universities sought social inclusion in the national transition to majority rule, but they also sought what Soudien refers to as 'epistemological hospitality', meaning a wide range of world views.

In practice, the ANC government was more concerned with ensuring the 'correct' political orientation of the universities than focussing on promoting those broader elements which determine a real university's character. This overriding bias toward African-isation of South Africa's universities led to early appointments of Vice Chancellors and senior staff sympathetic to the ANC's Africanist cause. This politicisation of higher learning has not only been damaging to the value of many South African degrees, but has resulted in a significant reduction in academic standards. At previously-Afrikaans universities, the elimination of Afrikaans as the language of instruction was always going to be a painful change for the incumbent staff.

The vehicle for change was the Employment Equity Act which aimed to dismantle 'white privilege'. The Act's focus was on race, although it also aimed to correct both gender and disability bias. Cultural transformation was given priority over intellectual standards and, as a result, considerable numbers of academics sought their future overseas while others retired early. The social dynamics of the universities changed and the personal advantages of conforming with ANC ideological goals of Africanisation became increasingly clear to all involved. The effects of racial emphasis were dramatic in the social sciences, arts and languages, but the hard sciences which underpinned engineering, maths, IT, science and medicine, could only be affected through the changed racial make-up of the student body. The extent to which 'soft marking' was encouraged by the need for African throughput is unknown, although suspicion was rife.

At the same time, it must be acknowledged that a quite remarkable group of African intellectual achievers were found by the ANC overseas to fill VC posts and professorships. Doubtless many ex-patriots could not be enticed home, but most of those who were, gave a credible injection of Black intelligentsia with international standing.

The most dramatic cultural changes occurred in the Afrikaans universities at Stellenbosch, Bloemfontein, Pretoria, Johannesburg and Potchefstroom. Whereas these had long been seats of Afrikaner Nationalism, in a matter of a decade they came to represent African

Nationalism – perhaps the world's starkest cultural transition of modern times. Describing these changes in such absolute terms may be an exaggeratio, because within each of these universities, notably Stellenbosch and Pretoria, there are pockets of a healthy comparative cultural contest of ideas which is the essence of a university's being.

The peaceful and positive achievement of mass cultural transition across all of a country's universities is no mean feat. However, the proof of the pudding is in the quality of the graduates, not only in their professionalism, but in their open-minded worldview. Unsurprisingly, many in the career professions now choose to seek their future offshore, as evidenced by the large numbers of medical, dental, financial and engineering migrants to other English-speaking countries. Thus while the university as an incubator of cultural identity and pride has its place in short term politics, racial dominance has no place in the modern university if it also values social cohesion, respect for diversity, tolerance of difference and multiculturism as life-enriching elements of modern society.

In Australia, the tertiary education sector has a proud record of both facilitating the entry of Aboriginal scholars into the professions, and of setting up Indigenous Study Centres as support organisations for students needing help in adapting to the wide world of inter-cultural academia. These centres can play a pivotal role in assisting students to choose the extent to which they want their individuality to be defined by their racial background. At the same time, as the leading Indigenous academic Marcia Langton has warned, these Indigenous Study Centres must avoid becoming 'refuges from reality' in the sense that they over-protect students by way of the inward-looking view of some Indigenous academics.

This narrow cultural exclusiveness does nothing to help young scholars adapt and transform into citizens of the world.

So far, Australia has resisted the temptation to establish a purely Aboriginal university although the Bachelor Institute in the Northern Territory comes close, albeit as an offshoot of Charles Darwin University. In the meantime, every effort is made to support and encourage Aboriginal professionals to act as role models to their people. Nothing gives more pride than the Aboriginal doctor or lawyer delivering their skilled services to their people. Long may they champion their cause by demonstrating that all that's needed is opportunity.

Conclusion

Perhaps it is useful to end this consideration of emerging new race relations in South Africa and Australia with a few observations from some big thinkers, starting with Nadine Gordimer. Her 1973 book, 'Black Interpreters', sketches the way in which African heroes, as portrayed in her comprehensive literature review, are individuals 'caught between two world views and two irreconcilable ideological demands'. These individuals seek the Whiteman's lifestyle and skills, but they also seek an existence which is 'no longer a contest between Indian and European'. They want, in Gordimer's view, 'to bring together in Africa, for Africa, the best of both worlds'. Those Africans who have produced autobiographies, she sees as benefitting from 'a catharsis for the sufferings of second-class citizens with first class brains'.

Students of Australian racial history will recognise Noel Pearson and Marcia Langton in this same category, but their minority's struggle is an emotional and moral struggle and not a political power play. These leaders are also operating in the dispossessed era of post-colonialism and its vivid living memories of exploitation. They don't seek refuge in bleeding-heart martyrdom; rather they ask only for a genuine 'fair go' so prized by those in the mainstream. They have overcome what has been referred to as 'the shock of watching themselves being erased' and have taken the best from two cultures, maintained their self-esteem of who they are, and have shown sufficient vision to demonstrate that grounded individuals can rise above former low expectations. They can do this through personal responsibility which drives them to exhibit their innate potential.

BIBLIOGRAPHY

Appia, K. (1996). Race, Culture and Identity. New Jersey: Princeton University Press.

Biko, S. (2004). I Write What I Like . Johannesburg: Picador.

Blum, J. (2015). In Mangcu, based on 'I'm Not a Racist but... Ithaca, N.Y. 2002: Cornell University Press.

Blum, L. (2007). Three Types of Race-related Solidarity. Journal of Social Philosophy 38 (1).

du Bois, W. (1903, reprint 1994). The Souls of Black Folk. New York: Dover Publications.

Everatt, D. (2009). The Origins of Non-Racialism. Johannesburg: Wits University Press.

Fanon, F. (1963). The Wretched Earth. New York: Grove Press.

Friedman, S. (2015). The Janus Face of the Past. Johannesburg: In Mangcu.

Gordimer, N. (1973). Black Interpreters. Johannesburg: Ravan Press.

Grant, S. (2015). Talking to My Country. Sydney: Harper Collins Publishing.

Hall, S. (1997). Race, the Floating Signifier . London: Goldsmith's College.

J.G., V. H. (1780). Reflections on the Philosophy of the History of Mankind . Chicago: University pf Chicago.

Jablonski, N. (XN). The Colour of Our Past and Present: The Evolution of Skin Pigmentation. Johannesburg: In Mangcu.

Langton, M. (2011). Support Centres Can Hold Back Indigenous Students. Sydney: The Australian, 20 April.

Mangcu, X. (2013). The Colour of Our Future. Johannesburg: Wits University Press.

Netshitenski, N. (2015). Interrogating the Concept and Dynamics of Race in Public Policy. Johannesburg: In Mangcu, p107.

Newman, C. J. (1909). The Idea of a University. New York: Harvard Classics, Collier Publishing.

North, D. (1990). Institutions, Institutional Change and Economic Performance. Cambridge, UK: Cambridge University Press.

Page, S. (2008). Path Dependence. University of Chicago: Q. Journal of Political Science 1:87, Now Publishers.

Pearson, N. (2014). A Rightful Place. Sydney: Quarterly Essay.

Pillay, S. (2015). Why I am no longer a Non-Racialist. Johannesburg: In Mangcu, p133.

Ross, D. (2015). Every Hill Got a Story.

Sandel, M. (1997). Democracy's Discontent. Cambridge, MA: Belknap Press.

Scott, D. (2004). Conscripts of Modernity. Durham, NC: Duke University Press.

Shelby, T. (2005). We Who Are Dark. Cambridge MA: Belknap Press.

Soudien, C. (2015). Interrogating Transformation in South African Higher Education. Johannesburg: In Mangcu, p153.

Professor Emeritus Brian Roberts has lived half his life in South Africa and half in Australia. An agricultural ecologist by profession, he has a passion for sustainable land use while his highly developed social conscience has led to decades of research into tribal peoples rights and responsibilities. Recognised as 'The Father of Landcare' he was awarded the Order of Australia in 1998, having earlier won the South African Community Service Medal for his work in rural soil conservation. He was the founding president of the Soil and Water Conservation Association of Australia, Organising Chairman of the Ninth International Rangeland Congress and has held professorships at three universities.

Professor Roberts chaired the Lower Balonne Advisory Committee on water sharing, the Queensland Rural Fires Council, the Queensland Freshwater MAC and the Nathan Dam Community Committee on Dawson River Water Supplies. As a senior member of the Cape York Peninsula Land Use Strategy and convenor of CSIRO's Water Quality Joint Venture team in North Queensland as Adjunct in Environmental Studies at James Cook University, he contributed to mainstream and Indigenous community conservation projects. He is a member of the National Conservation Advisory Committee and the Queensland Sheep and Wool Research Committee. Much of his recent writing has been published in Quadrant Online. He is the author of 13 books, many book chapters and numerous journal articles since 1956. As a member of ANU's Fundamental Questions program he produced the seminal paper 'Land Ethics: A necessary addition to Australian Values' (1984).

www.ingramcontent.com/pod-product-compliance
Lightning Source LLC
Chambersburg PA
CBHW032119020426
42334CB00016B/1011